"As a teacher of spiritual directors, I require my students to read *The Gift of Being Yourself* first. Understanding the false self and receiving the true self is essential for knowing God and one's truest desire, and it's a prerequisite for discerning this story in the lives of others. This new edition encourages readers to stop and consider the implications for themselves through questions and through examples from Benner's own life and the experiences of others. This calls for a careful consideration of Benner's premise as a lived reality, and not just as theory or ideas. I will highly recommend this edition for students of spiritual direction and formation."

**Helen Cepero,** spiritual director, author of *Christ-Shaped Character* and *Journaling as a Spiritual Practice*

"A small, engaging book on knowing God and knowing self. *The Gift of Being Yourself* gets beneath the crust of ego and past persona and behind image to the truth of you. Here is a pathway to discover and receive the beloved unrepeatable self that God designed you to be."

**Adele Calhoun,** author of *Spiritual Disciplines Handbook*

"In contrast to other books filled with drive-through pop psychology and sound-bite spirituality, Benner, a psychologist and spiritual director, offers an impressively deep and challenging introduction to Christian self-discovery in a little more than 100 pages. . . . He offers a clear and practical outline for those seeking to begin the lifelong process of knowing God and knowing themselves in an authentic way. . . . His discussion of accepting our flaws and sins as a necessary step to transformation is a model of lucidity. Although self-knowledge is the subject, it becomes clear that transformation is the ultimate goal both of this book and of the journey it invites readers to begin."

**Publishers Weekly** (starred review), January 26, 2004

"Wise, compassionate and accessible, David Benner's *The Gift of Being Yourself* is truly a gift to the dedicated seeker. The author draws on his professional experience as a psychologist and his own lifelong vocation as a Christian. The result is a book that felicitously weaves together the insights of psychology and Christian spirituality."

**Margaret Guenther,** author of *Holy Listening: The Art of Spiritual Direction*

"David Benner's *The Gift of Being Yourself* is the best treatment of the journey to becoming one's true self that I have ever read. I began reading the book as a favor to David; I finished it in one four-hour sitting as a favor to me. Drawing from his wisdom as a psychotherapist and spiritual director, insights from Scripture, and his own self and God discoveries, David gently describes the great disparity between the false self that most of us have become and the self-in-Christ that we are intended to be. I have never been so challenged and warmly inspired to receive the gift of being my true self."

**Gary W. Moon,** director, Martin Family Institute and Dallas Willard Center for Spiritual Formation at Westmont College, author of *Apprenticeship with Jesus*

"David Benner is a keen student of both God and human personhood. It is a rare kind of book that combines wisdom about faith and understanding about the self. This is that kind of book."

**John Ortberg,** author and senior pastor, Menlo Park Presbyterian Church, Menlo Park, California

"Slowly we are unpacking the full implications of incarnation. David Benner does exactly the same in this excellent book, using good theology, psychology and spiritual practice to make the profound obvious. This is the work of all good teachers."

**Richard Rohr, OFM,** Center for Action and Contemplation, Albuquerque, New Mexico

"As he has done many times before, David Benner guides us to a place of wisdom and devotion with this beautiful book. With empathy and insight he demonstrates that the two great tasks of life—knowing God and knowing ourselves—converge into a single adventure as we are drawn into the arms of our loving God."

**Mark R. McMinn,** Rech Professor of Psychology, Wheaton College, and author of *Why Sin Matters*

"Rarely do I suggest a book in spiritual direction with the exception of the sacred Scriptures. However, *The Gift of Being Yourself* I would offer to directees with enthusiasm. David Benner has shown us where life experience, personal insight and prayer meet: in God. I highly recommend it, especially for people beginning in spiritual direction."

**David I. Donovan, SJ,** Provincial Assistant for Formation, New England Province of the Society of Jesus

# The Spiritual Journey

When applied to the spiritual life, the metaphor of a journey is both helpful and somewhat misleading. Helpfully it reflects the fact that the essence of spirituality is a process—specifically, a process of transformation. Unhelpfully it obscures the fact that we are already what we seek and where we long to arrive—specifically, in God. Once we realize this, the nature of the journey reveals itself to be more one of awakening than accomplishment, more one of spiritual awareness than spiritual achievement.

There are, however, two very good reasons to describe the spiritual life in terms of a journey. First, it fits well with our experience. We are aware that the self that begins the spiritual journey is not the same as the one that ends it. The changes in identity and consciousness—how we understand what it means to be me and our inner experience of passing through life—are both sufficiently profound as to be best described as transformational. The same is true for the changes in our capacity for love and the functioning of our will and desires.

The second reason is that the spiritual journey involves following a path. Much more than adopting a set of beliefs, a path is a practice or set of practices that will characterize our whole life. Following this path is the way we participate in our transformation. It is the way we journey into God and, as we do, discover that all along we have already been in God. It is the way our identity, consciousness and life become grounded in our self-in-God and God's self-in-us.

Christian spirituality is taking on the mind and heart of Christ as we recognize Christ as the deepest truth of our being. It is actualizing the Christ who is in us. It is becoming fully and deeply human. It is experiencing and responding to the world through the mind and heart of God as we align ourselves with God's transformational agenda of making all things new in Christ. It is participating in the very life of God.

This trilogy describes the foundational Christian practice of surrender, how this practice emerges as a response to Perfect Love, and the changes this produces in our identity, will and deepest desires. Each of the three books focuses on one of these strands while interweaving it with the others. Together they serve as a manual for walking the spiritual path as God's heart and mind slowly but truly become our own. The Spiritual Journey trilogy includes:

*Surrender to Love: Discovering the Heart of Christian Spirituality*
*The Gift of Being Yourself: The Sacred Call to Self-Discovery*
*Desiring God's Will: Aligning Our Hearts with the Heart of God*

# THE GIFT OF
# BEING YOURSELF

*The Sacred Call to Self-Discovery*

*Expanded Edition*

## DAVID G. BENNER

*Foreword by* M. BASIL PENNINGTON

IVP Books

An imprint of InterVarsity Press
Downers Grove, Illinois

InterVarsity Press
P.O. Box 1400, Downers Grove, IL 60515-1426
ivpress.com
email@ivpress.com

Expanded Edition ©2015 by David G. Benner
First Edition ©2004 by David G. Benner

InterVarsity Press® is the book-publishing division of InterVarsity Christian Fellowship/USA®, a movement of students and faculty active on campus at hundreds of universities, colleges and schools of nursing in the United States of America, and a member movement of the International Fellowship of Evangelical Students. For information about local and regional activities, visit intervarsity.org.

Scripture is taken from the Jerusalem Bible, copyright © 1966 by Darton, Longman & Todd, Ltd. and Doubleday, a division of Bantam Doubleday Dell Publishing Group, Inc. Reprinted by permission.

While any stories in this book are true, some names and identifying information may have been changed to protect the privacy of individuals.

Cover design: Cindy Kiple
Interior design: Beth McGill
Images: Cock Pheasant tapestry, made by Morris & Co., John Henry Dearle / Birmingham Museums and Art
    Gallery / Bridgeman Images

ISBN 978-0-8308-4612-2 (print)
ISBN 978-0-8308-9945-6 (digital)

Printed in the United States of America ∞

**green press** *As a member of the Green Press Initiative, InterVarsity Press is committed to protecting*
**INITIATIVE** *the environment and to the responsible use of natural resources. To learn more, visit*
*greenpressinitiative.org.*

**Library of Congress Cataloging-in-Publication Data**
Benner, David G.
    The gift of being yourself : the sacred call to self-discovery / David G. Benner. -- Expanded Edition
        pages cm. -- (The spiritual journey)
    Includes bibliographical references.
    ISBN 978-0-8308-4612-2 (pbk. : alk. paper)
    1. Spiritual life--Christianity. 2. Self-realization--Religious aspects--Christianity. I. Title.
    BV4501.3.B457 2015
    248.4--dc23
                                                                                                    2015022996

**P**  21  20  19  18  17  16  15  14  13  12  11  10  9  8  7  6  5  4  3  2  1

**Y**  33  32  31  30  29  28  27  26  25  24  23  22  21  20  19  18  17  16  15

To

Gary Moon

and

Jeff and DeAnne Terrell

*There is only one problem on which all my existence,*

*my peace, and my happiness depend:*

*to discover myself in discovering God.*

*If I find Him I will find myself*

*and if I find my true self I will find Him.*

THOMAS MERTON

# Contents

# Foreword

*by Dom M. Basil Pennington, OSCO*

*I* number reading Dr. David Benner's previous volume, *Surrender to Love,* among the great graces of my life. Now the doctor gifts us with another slim, powerful volume. Benner's writing is powerful here, as elsewhere, because it comes out of deep personal experience that he courageously shares with his readers. He writes credibly of God because, as he says, he knows God, and "God is the only context in which [our] being makes sense." And again, in his eminently practical and compassionate way, Benner shows us step by step how to enter into the wisdom he shares.

One of the retirement projects I had assigned myself (when retirement was far off!) was to take in the rich insights of some of the great theological thinkers of our times—Bernard Lonergan, Pierre Teilhard de Chardin, John Dunne—and re-present them in simpler terms that would make them more readily accessible to the ordinary reader so that they could impact his or her life. Without realizing it, David Benner has done something of this, making accessible to us in a most readable but no less rich text some of the exciting insight of Teilhard de Chardin—I think here especially of *The Divine Milieu*. The all-pervasive immanence of God, who ever brings us forth in his creative love and is with us in all we do, is given immediate pastoral significance. Reading this volume, one's mind cannot but jump forward to embracing the sacredness of all human life with its practical implications in regard to abortion, so-called mercy killing, the death penalty, weaponry and war, ecological care so that our planet will sustain the next generations, and the appropriate sharing of what we now have to sustain life in this generation.

Some will also perceive that Benner is giving us a very enriching companion text for what is probably the most powerful spiritual program developed in the last century, the Twelve-Step Program, now adapted to so many of our deepest ills. Any older person with the insight that comes with years and especially retirement finds himself convicted of having in some ways lived the "lie that grew from the soil of self-ignorance."

The doctor assails us again and again with one-liners that hit home with painful accuracy. Startling sentences jump out to inscribe themselves in our memory and continuously call us forth into truth:

> Our challenge is to unmask the Divine in the natural and name the presence of God in our lives.

> Created from love, of love and for love, our existence makes no sense apart from Divine love.

> If God loves and accepts you as a sinner, how can you do less?

> Self-acceptance always precedes genuine self-surrender and self-transformation.

> We believe we know how to take care of our needs better than God.

We all tend to fashion a god who fits our falsity.

We do not find our true self by seeking it. Rather, we find it by seeking God.

Jesus is the True Self who shows us by his life how to find our self in relation to God.

Our happiness is important to God.

—just to list a few.

This is a very challenging book. If we do listen to it fully and seek to implement it in our life, it will lead to a transformation. That will mean the death of our carefully cultivated false self. This hurts, to say the very least. If I were sinless, the perfect image of God, I could know the God of love. But knowing myself as the sinner enables me to know something more: a God of mercy—something greater, for love responds to what is good and lovable; mercy responds to what is not good and makes it good and lovable, the gift of being myself.

David's book has just begun to do its work within me. I shall spend many hours with it, hours that I trust will be very fruitful. And I hope that will be your experience also.

# Identity and Authenticity

*I*t is a profound irony to write a book promoting self-discovery to people who are seeking to follow a self-sacrificing Christ. It might well make you fear that I have forgotten—or worse, failed to take seriously—Jesus' paradoxical teaching that it is in losing our self that we truly find it (Matthew 10:39). As you read on I think you will see that I have done neither.

While concepts such as self-discovery, identity and authenticity are easily dismissed as mere psychobabble, each has an important role to play in the transformational journey of Christian spirituality. Even in the Matthew passage just referenced, Jesus talks as much about self-discovery as self-sacrifice! But there is no question that the journey of finding our truly authentic self in Christ and rooting our identity in this reality is dramatically different from the agenda of self-fulfillment promoted by pop psychology.

The absurdity of a pop psychology approach to the self is epitomized in a cartoon I recently saw. Addressing a stranger at a party, a woman says, "I don't know anybody here but the hostess—and, of course, in a much deeper sense, myself." Quite obviously, there are many profoundly non-Christian and often quite ridiculous ways of pursuing self-discovery and authenticity!

Still, Christian spirituality has a great deal to do with the self, not just with God. The goal of the spiritual journey is the transformation of self. As we shall see, this requires knowing both our self and God. Both are necessary if we are to discover our true identity as those who are "in Christ" (2 Corinthians 5:17), because the self is where we meet God. Both are also necessary if we are to live out the uniqueness of our vocation.

In all of creation, identity is a challenge only for humans. A tulip knows exactly what it is. It is never tempted by false ways of being. Nor does it face complicated decisions in the process of becoming. So it is with dogs, rocks, trees, stars, amoebas, electrons and all other things. All give glory to God by being exactly what they are. For in being what God means them to be, they are obeying him. Humans, however, encounter a more challenging existence. We think. We consider options. We decide. We act. We doubt. Simple being is tremendously difficult to achieve and fully authentic being is extremely rare.

Body and soul contain thousands of possibilities out of which you can build many identities. But in only one of these will you find your true self that has been hidden in Christ from all eternity. Only in one will you discover your unique vocation and deepest fulfillment. But, as Dag Hammarskjöld argues, you will never find this "until you have excluded all those superficial and fleeting possibilities of being and doing with which you toy out of curiosity or wonder or greed, and which hinder you from casting anchor in the experience of the mystery of life, and the consciousness of the talent entrusted to you which is your I."[1]

We all live searching for that one possible way of being that carries with it the gift of authenticity. We are most conscious of this search for identity during adolescence, when it takes front stage. At this stage of life we try on identities like clothing, looking for a style of being that fits with how we want to be seen. But even long after adolescence has passed, most adults know the occasional feeling of being a fraud—a sense of being not what they pretend to be but rather precisely what they pretend *not* to be. With a little reflection, most of us can become aware of masks that we first adopted as strategies to avoid feelings of vulnerability but that have become parts of our social self. Tragically, we settle easily for pretense, and a truly authentic self often seems illusory.

There is, however, a way of being for each of us that is as natural and deeply congruent as the life of the tulip. Beneath the roles and masks lies a possibility of a self that is as unique as a snowflake. It is an originality that has existed since God first loved us into existence. Our true self-in-Christ is the only self that will support authenticity. It and it alone provides an identity that is eternal.

Finding that unique self is, as noted by Thomas Merton, the problem on which all our existence, peace and happiness depend.[2] Nothing is more important, for if we find our true self we find God, and if we find God, we find our most authentic self.

## BECOMING YOUR TRUE SELF

Being yourself would not make any spiritual sense if your uniqueness were not of immense value to God. But each person is exactly that—of inestimable value to God.

We should never be tempted to think that growth in Christlikeness reduces our uniqueness. While some Christian visions of the spiritual life imply that as we become more like Christ we look more and more like each other, such a cultic expectation of loss of individuality has nothing in common with genuine Christian spirituality. Paradoxically, as we become more and more like Christ we become more uniquely our own true self.

As we shall see in what follows, there are many false ways of achieving uniqueness. These all result from attempts to *create* a self rather than *receive* the gift of my self-in-Christ. But the uniqueness that comes from being our true self is not a uniqueness of our own making. Identity is never simply a creation. It is always a discovery. True identity is always a gift of God.

The desire for uniqueness is a spiritual desire. So too is the longing to be authentic. These are not simply psychological longings, irrelevant to the spiritual journey. Both are the response of spirit to Spirit—the Holy Spirit calling us home to our place and identity in God.

Being most deeply your unique self is something that God desires, because your true self is grounded in Christ. God created you in uniqueness and seeks to restore you to that uniqueness in Christ. Finding and living out your true self is fulfilling your destiny.

This book is about the transformational journey of becoming our true self-in-Christ and living out the vocation that this involves. After the case for the interdependence of knowing God and self is laid out in chapter one, the book is organized around three broad needs faced by all Christians who seek to put themselves at God's disposal:

1. The need for a transformational knowing of God that comes from meeting God in the depths of our beings. This is the focus of chapter two.

2. The need for a transformational knowing of ourselves that comes from discovering how we are known by God. This is the focus of chapters three, four and five. (Devoting three chapters to knowing self and only one to knowing God does not mean that I think knowing self is more important than knowing God. It reflects the fact that while there are thousands of books on knowing God, very little is written on the role of knowing self in Christian spirituality. Also, because of the interdependence of these two forms of knowing, we will repeatedly encounter ways of knowing God throughout the chapters that explore ways of knowing self.)

3. The need to find our identity, fulfillment and vocation in our hidden self in Christ—the focus of chapter six.

The transformational journey is not as linear as this implies, so actually the discussion will weave back and forth among these topics. Furthermore, the dimensions of the journey are interrelated. As we shall see, true knowing of our self demands that we know our self as known by God, and true knowing of God demands that we know God not just as an abstraction or as objective data but in and through our lived experience.

I pray that what follows will help you discover the uniqueness of who you were called from eternity to be. I trust that it will help you know both yourself and God more deeply, and thus discover the gift of truly being yourself.

*Sydney, Australia*
*Fourth Thursday of Lent*

# one

# Transformational
# Knowing of Self and God

*I*n the epigraph that opens this book, Thomas Merton tells us
what he considers the most important thing in the whole
world—that on which his entire existence, happiness and peace
depend. What would you identify as the most important thing for
your existence and well-being? How do you think most Christians
you know would answer the question?

Many Christians I know would answer with two words: "Finding
God." Others might use the language of knowing, loving and
serving God. Some would include the church or relationships with
other people in their answer. However they would express it, I
suspect that most Christians would say something about God but
would not make any reference to self.

To suggest that knowing God plays an important role in Christian
spirituality will not surprise anyone. To suggest that knowing self
plays an equally important role will set off warning bells for many
people—being perhaps just the sort of thing you might expect from
an author who is a psychologist, not a theologian.

Yet an understanding of the interdependence of knowing self

and God has held a lasting and respected place in Christian theology. Thomas à Kempis argued that "a humble self-knowledge is a surer way to God than a search after deep learning,"[1] and Augustine's prayer was "Grant, Lord, that I may know myself that I may know thee."[2] These are but a small sample of the vast number of theologians who have held this position since the earliest days of the church.

Christian spirituality involves a transformation of the self that occurs only when God and self are both deeply known. Both, therefore, have an important place in Christian spirituality. There is no deep knowing of God without a deep knowing of self, and no deep knowing of self without a deep knowing of God. John Calvin wrote, "Nearly the whole of sacred doctrine consists in these two parts: knowledge of God and of ourselves."[3]

Though there has never been any serious theological quarrel with this ancient Christian understanding, it has been largely forgotten by the contemporary church. We have focused on knowing God and tended to ignore knowing ourselves. The consequences have often been grievous—marriages betrayed, families destroyed, ministries shipwrecked and endless numbers of people damaged.

Leaving the self out of Christian spirituality results in a spirituality that is not well grounded in experience. It is, therefore, not well grounded in reality. Focusing on God while failing to know ourselves deeply may produce an external form of piety, but it will always leave a gap between appearance and reality. This is dangerous to the soul of anyone—and in spiritual leaders it can also be disastrous for those they lead.

Consider the way a lack of self-knowledge affected the life of a well-known pastor and his congregation. No one would have doubted this man's knowing of God—at least before his very public downfall. He had built a very successful ministry around his preaching, and there was no reason to suspect that he did not personally know the truths he publicly proclaimed. Nor was there any obvious reason to question his knowing of himself. Anyone who thought about the matter would probably have judged his self-understanding to be deep. His sermons often included significant self-disclosure, and he seemed to know how to be vulnerable before God.

But as for many of us, all of that was more appearance than reality. The self this pastor showed to the world was a public self he had crafted with great care—a false self of his own creation. Between this public self and his true experience lay an enormous chasm. Both that chasm and his inner experience lay largely outside his awareness.

Suddenly the gap between his inner reality and external appearance was exposed. Things that he did not know or accept about himself welled up within him and shattered the illusion his life represented. Lust led to sexual involvement with a woman he was counseling, just as greed had earlier led to misuse of church funds. As these things became public, the lie that was his life imploded. It was a lie he had lived before his family, closest friends, congregation, God and himself. It was a lie that grew from the soil of self-ignorance.

There is no need to identify this man, nor even to give him a fictitious name. His story is all too familiar. He reminds us of Jesus' teaching about the dangers of the blind leading the blind (Matthew 15:14)—both easily falling into a pit of pain and despair. Just how serious is this? According to Jesus, it is better to be thrown into the sea with a millstone about your neck than to cause one person to stumble in such a manner (Matthew 18:6). This pastor, and many others like him, have caused not just one but thousands to stumble and left them with devastating wounds.

## KNOWLEDGE THAT FILLS

This man was not short on knowledge about either himself or God.

But none of it did him any good. None of it was worthy of being called *transformational knowing*.

Not all knowledge transforms. Some merely puffs us up like an overfilled balloon. And you know what happens to overfilled balloons!

Actor and filmmaker Woody Allen often speaks publicly of his decades in psychoanalysis—three or four sessions per week on a couch, saying whatever came into his mind, allowing his analyst's periodic interpretations of the meaning of these free associations to guide his exploration. However, there is little evidence that Allen's self-knowledge has brought him freedom or psychological health. In fact, making his continuing neurotic struggles the hallmark of his public character, he often focuses his sardonic humor on the limits of self-understanding as a means of change.

Self-knowledge that is pursued apart from knowing our identity in relationship to God easily leads to self-inflation. This is the puffed-up, grandiose self Paul warns about (1 Corinthians 8:1)—an arrogance to which we are vulnerable when knowledge is valued more than love. It can also lead to self-preoccupation. Unless we spend as much time looking at God as we spend looking at our self, our knowing of our self will simply draw us further and further into an abyss of self-fixation.

But it is also quite possible to be stuffed with knowledge about God that does nothing to help us genuinely know either God or self. Having information about God is no more transformational than having information about love. Theories and ideas about God can sit in sturdy storage canisters in our mind and do absolutely no good. If you doubt this, recall Jesus' harsh words for the religious leaders of his day who knew God's law but did not know God's heart.

The pastor whose story I just told had a great deal of information about God. He also seemed to know lots of things about himself. But this knowledge was all objective, not personal. It was, therefore, relatively useless to him.

He told me, for example, that he knew God is forgiving. But he had never really experienced this forgiveness, at least not in relation to any significant failure. It would be more accurate to say that he *believed* God is forgiving but did not *know* this as an experiential truth. Living the lie of his pretend self, he had always taken safe, inconsequential sins to God for forgiveness, never daring to expose the reality of his inner world to God. To do so would have required that he face this reality himself. That he had never been prepared to do.

He told me that his enemy was sloth—spiritual laziness. He said he had often asked God to forgive him for not working harder for the kingdom. But confession of such a sin was nothing more than a distraction. It kept his focus (and, perhaps he hoped, God's focus) off the deeper things about himself that were so profoundly disordered.

He also told me that he knew God is love. But again, this was a belief, not an experience. To truly know love, we must receive it in an undefended state—in the vulnerability of a "just as I am" encounter. This man had never been able to allow himself this degree of vulnerability with anyone—not his wife, nor his children, nor his closest friends, and certainly not God.

Not surprisingly, then, his knowledge of himself was equally superficial. Listening to the things he told me about his life was like reading a throwaway paperback novel or watching a B-grade movie. The role he was playing lacked depth and reality. It was two-dimensional. As he told me about himself he was describing someone he had been watching from a distance. The knowledge he had of this person was objective and remote. It had, therefore, no transformational value. It was simply his pitiful attempt to give flesh-and-bones reality to the falsity of his pretend self. The self he sought to project to the world was an illusion.

Even after his crisis, this man had enormous difficulty being honest. His longstanding, deeply ingrained tendency to present a pretend, idealized self survived the dissolution of both his ministry and his marriage. It wasn't so much that he told lies as that he lived them. This is the tragedy of the false self. But unfortunately, this man did not have a monopoly on falsity. It is a part of all of us, to one degree or another.

## Knowledge That Transforms

Truly transformational knowledge is always personal, never merely objective. It involves *knowing of,* not merely *knowing about*. And it is always relational. It grows out of a relationship to the object that is known—whether this is God or one's self.

Objective knowing can occur in relation to anything that we examine at a distance. It is knowing that is independent of us. For example, you may know that Earth orbits around the sun or that Columbus arrived in the Americas in 1492 without direct personal experience of either, provided you are willing to accept the testimony of others. This is how it is with much of what we believe.

Personal knowing, on the other hand, is based on experience. It is therefore subjective. I know that my wife loves me because of my experience of her. While I can describe her love to someone else, I cannot prove it. I cannot make it objective. Yet this does not detract from the validity of my knowing.

Because personal knowing is based on experience, it requires that we be open to the experience. Knowing God's love demands that we receive God's love—experientially, not simply as a theory. Personal knowledge is never simply a matter of the head. Because it is rooted in experience, it is grounded in deep places in our being. The things we know from experience we know beyond belief. Such knowing is not incompatible with belief, but it is not dependent on it.

I do not merely believe that my wife loves me, I know she loves me. And as arrogant as it may sound, I can say that I do not merely believe in God, I know God—certainly not exhaustively, but none-theless genuinely.

People who have never developed a deep personal knowing of God will be limited in the depth of their personal knowing of themselves. Failing to know God, they will be unable to know themselves, as God is the only context in which their being makes sense. Similarly, people who are afraid to look deeply at themselves will of course be equally afraid to look deeply at God. For such persons, ideas about God provide a substitute for direct experience of God.

Knowing God and knowing self are therefore interdependent. Neither can proceed very far without the other. Paradoxically, we come to know God best not by looking at God exclusively, but by looking at God and then looking at ourselves—then looking at God, and then again looking at ourselves. This is also the way we best come to know our selves. Both God and self are mostly fully known in relationship to each other.

## PETER'S TRANSFORMATIONAL KNOWING

To illustrate how this unfolds, consider the spiritual journey of Peter. The rock on which Christ promised to build his church was remarkably crumbly. But none of the disciples showed more growth in understanding of both self and God during the three years of accompanying Christ.

Let us look in on Peter's inner knowing at several points on this journey. The first of these is his initial meeting of Christ and Christ's call to follow him. What might we assume that Peter knew about himself and God at this point?

Andrew, Peter's brother, met Jesus first, right away accepting the invitation to follow him. Andrew then went to Peter, told him that he had found the Messiah and brought Peter to Jesus to see for himself. Peter's response was the same as that of his brother—he immediately left his fishing nets to follow Jesus (Matthew 4:18-22). From this account it seems safe to assume that Peter accepted Jesus as the Messiah. If so, we could say that he believed that Jesus was the long-hoped-for deliverer from the oppression of the Romans. At this point this knowing was a belief—a hope based on the conviction of his brother and his own brief contact with Jesus.

But what might he have known about himself? I am speculating, of course, but perhaps if asked about himself he might have told us that he was a fisherman. Possibly, he might have added that he was somewhat hot-tempered and impulsive. And perhaps he would have told us about his longing for a savior for his people—and this would show that he was a man of hope and faith. It is, however, highly unlikely that he could have known the depths of his fears or the magnitude of his pride. These levels of knowing of self awaited deeper knowing of God.

Moving ahead to his encounter with Jesus walking on the water (Matthew 14:22-33), it seems reasonable to assume that by now Peter's belief that Jesus was the Christ would have been even more solid. Peter had witnessed Jesus' numerous miracles, had heard him preach to large crowds and dialogue with individuals, and had had opportunity to watch him closely.

But on this night, Peter was not thinking about any of this. Out in a boat in the midst of a severe storm, Peter and the other disciples were preoccupied with their immediate safety. Suddenly seeing Jesus walking on the water toward them, they were terrified.

Jesus' words to them must have been instantly reassuring: "Courage! It is I! Do not be afraid."

Peter immediately cried out in response, "If it is you, tell me to come to you across the water."

Christ invited him to step out of the boat and come to him, and Peter did just that.

If asked what he now knew of God after this experience, Peter might tell of his increasing conviction that Jesus was indeed the Christ. He might also speak of his developing hope based on witnessing Christ's miracles. He might say that he felt reassured in knowing that God had heard the prayers of his people and had at last sent their Redeemer.

Asked what he knew of himself, he might be able now to speak of his fears. While he had the courage to step out on the waters at Christ's bidding, he also experienced the terror of beginning to sink when he looked at the waves rather than Christ. But—he would likely quickly add—this had only served to increase his trust in Christ.

Jumping ahead to Jesus' washing of the disciples' feet (John 13), we see Peter's initial refusal to allow Christ to wash his feet followed by Christ's prediction of Peter's betrayal. What might Peter have said of his knowing of God and self at this point?

It seems probable that Peter might now speak with confidence about his love of Jesus, the fervency of his belief that Jesus was the Christ, and his utter disbelief and shock at Jesus' prediction of his impending denial of him. This matter of the denial must have left him profoundly puzzled. It must have been inconceivable to him that he could ever deny Jesus. Did Jesus not know the depths of his love? Did he not know of his heroic courage and the strength of his convictions? He must have assumed that Christ was mistaken in this prediction. Doubting Jesus was easier than doubting himself. He had not yet encountered either his pride or the extent of his fear.

Briefly looking in on Peter after his denial of Christ (John 18:15-27), we would probably find him self-absorbed in regret and anguish. In a moment he had been confronted by his lack of courage, his treasonous lack of loyalty and the depths of his fears. He might also be thinking about how easily his pride had been wounded by Jesus' prediction of his denial. Perhaps he was also remembering his protestation that "even if all lose faith, I will not" (Mark 14:29).

In short, he had encountered his weakest and most despicable self, and he was likely filled with self-loathing.

Finally, what can we say about Peter's knowing of himself and God at the point of his encounter with the risen Christ (John 21:15-25)? After the death of Christ, Peter and a number of the other disciples had gone back to fishing. What else was left? After a night of catching absolutely nothing, they met an unknown person on the shore in the early dawn, a man who asked about their catch and encouraged them to try casting the net on the other side of the boat. Immediately their nets were filled to overflowing with fish. And immediately they recognized their Lord. Peter quickly leaped overboard and began swimming toward shore.

Mirroring the pattern of his denials, Jesus asked him three times if he loved him more than the other disciples. This gave Peter three chances to declare his love—one for each denial. Jesus' response was to repeat his invitation for Peter to follow him (John 21:19), precisely the same invitation that had begun their relationship.

What might Peter tell us at this point about his knowing of God and himself? I suspect he would have first said how little he had truly known either himself or Jesus prior to this. With regard to Jesus, I suspect he would repeat with amazement how forgiving Jesus was. What he had known as objective information from witnessing Jesus' encounters with others, he now knew deeply and personally. And I am sure he would have spoken of his new level of readiness to follow the Christ whom he now knew in his heart, not just his mind.

The interweaving of the deepening knowledge of self and God that we have seen in Peter's experience illustrates the way genuine knowing of God and self occurs. Peter could not truly know Jesus apart from knowing himself in relation to Jesus. He did not know himself until Jesus showed him who he was. But in learning about himself, he also came to truly know Jesus.

Deep knowing of God and deep knowing of self always develop interactively. The result is the authentic transformation of the self that is at the core of Christian spirituality.

## THE DIVINE INVITATION

What have you learned about yourself as a result of your experience with God? And what do you know about God as a result of genuine encounter with your self?

The first thing many Christians would say they know about themselves as a result of their relationship with God is their sinfulness. And quite possibly the first thing they would say they learned about God from this was God's forgiveness and love. These are important things to know, and I will have more to say about them in future chapters. But what else do you know about yourself and God that has arisen from your encounter with the Divine?

While many of us have followed Jesus for much longer than the three years we have tracked in Peter's journey, too often we have not allowed the initial introduction to deepen into a deep, intimate knowing. Though we glibly talk about a personal relationship with God, many of us know God less well than we know our casual acquaintances. Too easily we have settled for knowing *about* God. Too easily our actual relationship with God is remarkably superficial. Is it any surprise, then, that we haven't learned very much about our self as a result of this encounter?

If this is your experience, don't allow yourself to be distracted by guilt. Hear God's call to a deep personal encounter as an invitation, not a reprimand. It is an invitation to step out of the security of your boat and meet Jesus in the vulnerability and chaos of your inner storms. It is an invitation to move beyond objective knowledge to personal knowing. It is an invitation to truly know God.

# two

# Knowing God

*I*t is easy to be dishonest in speaking of knowing God. So often our cliché-ridden God-talk is seriously out of touch with our actual experience.

I am hoping that my friendship with Vicki will help me avoid this. In my imagination she is sitting beside me as I write this chapter, reading over my shoulder.

Vicki wants to know God more than anything in the world. This has been her deepest longing for more than a decade of Christ-following. It is such a deep longing that she refuses to accept any substitute—especially the lies that she knows could easily roll off her tongue if she used the language of "personal relationship with God" to apply to her own experience. She feels very alone, fearing that she has somehow failed to do something right or that she is in some deep way defective and incapable of experiencing God. But she is not nearly as alone as she feels. She is simply more honest. And her yearning for intimacy with God is more passionate.

J. I. Packer suggests that knowing becomes increasingly complex as we move from knowing objects to knowing people and from knowing people to knowing God: "The more complex the object, the more complex is the knowing of it."[1] So since genuinely knowing another human is itself a demanding task, knowing the invisible God might seem utterly impossible. It would be if it were not for the fact that it is something God desires more deeply than we ever possibly could.

It is quite astounding that God wants to be known by human beings. But nothing gives God more pleasure (Hosea 6:6). Revelation is fundamental to the Divine character. God longs to disclose to us.

Revelation is not simply something that happened at some distant point in the past. If it were, all we could ever hope for is information from this historic event. But "God has no more stopped being Revelation than he has stopped being Love."[2] The good news is that God can be known by human beings, personally and experientially. This is the essence of eternal life (John 17:3). There is nothing in the whole world of greater value (Philippians 3:7-10).

But what is this knowing of God that is of supreme value, that gives God such pleasure, and that gives us genuine and eternal life? It is personal knowing—knowing that begins with belief but is deepened through relationship.

Many of the things we know about God we know objectively, accepting them as facts on the trusted testimony of Scriptures and the community of faith. These ground our more personal knowing, serving as an anchor in times of doubt and a frame of reference for making sense of our experience. This bedrock of beliefs will be elaborated by experience but never replaced by it. God's intention is that we know Divine love by experiencing it. But even when our Divine Lover seems distant, we can hold confident to the hope of the steadfast nature of God's love because of the testimony of Scriptures and the witness of others.

As valuable as this objective knowing is, Packer reminds us that even "a little knowledge *of* God is worth more than a great deal of

knowledge *about* Him."[3] Transformational knowing of God comes
from the intimate, personal knowing of Divine love. Because God
is love, God can only be known through love. To know God is to
love God, and to love God is to know God (1 John 4:7-8). The
Christian God is known only in devotion, not objective detachment.
This is why Paul's prayer is that we may know the love of Christ
and so be filled with the utter fullness of God (Ephesians 3:19).
This is transformational knowing.

Knowing God also requires surrender. Thomas Merton writes
that "we must know the truth, we must love the truth we know and
we must act according to the measure of our love. Truth is God
himself who cannot be known apart from love and cannot be loved
apart from surrender to his will."[4] Genuine knowing demands a
response. To know God demands that we be willing to be touched
by Divine love. To be touched by God's love is to be forever
changed. To surrender to Divine love is to find our soul's home—
the place and identity for which we yearn in every cell of our being.

### Knowing Jesus

If the invisible God had never become visible, our knowing of God
would remain very limited. But Divine self-revelation was made
complete in Jesus. To know Jesus, therefore, is to know God (John
14:9). Jesus is the "image of the invisible God" (Colossians 1:15
NRSV). Thus he is the filter through which we need to pass all our
ideas about God as we seek to move from knowing about God to
meeting God personally in Jesus.

Some Christians speak of a personal encounter with Jesus as if
this were a one-time matter—something that happens at conversion. This is a tragic confusion of an introduction and a relationship. A first encounter is just that—a first encounter. What
God longs for us to experience is intimate knowing that comes by
means of an ongoing relationship.

Think again of Peter to see how relationship with Jesus enhances knowing of God. As a first-century Palestinian Jew, Peter would have known a number of things about God before his encounter with Jesus. This knowing would have been based on being part of a believing community that constantly shared stories of God's mighty dealings with them over their history. He would have known, for example, that God was the Creator of all things. He would also have known that God had rescued his ancestors from bondage in Egypt. And he would have known that this God of Abraham, Isaac and Jacob was a holy God.

But all of this objective knowing was dramatically enhanced as Peter came to know Jesus. His two epistles are filled with personal knowing of God that came from spending three years of his life with Jesus. This relationship-based knowing introduced Peter to a God he could never have known apart from Jesus. Consider just a few of the things he learned, found in his first epistle:

- God is the source of new life and a living hope that is based in the resurrected Christ (1 Peter 1:3)

- God is the source of a faith that is more precious than gold (1 Peter 1:7)

- God is a fountain of inexpressible joy (1 Peter 1:8)

- God judges with fairness and impartiality (1 Peter 1:17)

- God allows us to share Christ's sufferings as a way of knowing Jesus through identification (1 Peter 4:12-13)

- God is faithful and can be trusted to do what is right (1 Peter 4:19)

- God is opposed to the proud but gives grace to the humble (1 Peter 5:6)

Reading Peter's epistles makes me wonder if this is the same hotheaded fisherman we meet in the Gospels! Something dramatic has happened to him. His knowing of both God and his own self underwent a radical change because he came to know Jesus.

Relationships develop when people spend time together. Spending time with God ought to be the essence of prayer. However, as it is usually practiced, prayer is more like a series of email or instant messages than hanging out together. Often it involves more talking than listening. It should not be a surprise that the result is a superficial relationship.

The starting point for learning to simply spend time with God is learning to do this with Jesus. Spending time with Jesus allows us to ground our God-knowing in the concrete events of a concrete life. But how do we actually do this? We do it by means of Spirit-guided meditation on the Gospels.

## Meeting Jesus in the Gospels

Gospel meditation provides an opportunity to enter specific moments in Jesus' life and thereby share his experience. Shared experience is the core of any friendship. And Spirit-guided meditation on the life of Jesus provides this possibility.

The meditation I am recommending is not the same as Bible study. It is more an exercise of the imagination than of the intellect. It involves allowing the Spirit of God to help you imaginatively enter an event in the life of Christ as presented in the Gospels.

Let me illustrate what I mean by this by suggesting a simple exercise based on Mark's account of Jesus and the rich young man.

First, take a moment to quiet yourself in God's presence. Close your eyes and ask God to take the words of Scripture and, by the power of his Spirit, make them God's Word to you. Ask for the gift of a few moments of Spirit-guided imaginative encounter with Jesus. Then slowly read the following account several times—preferably out loud.

[Jesus] was setting out on a journey when a man ran up, knelt before him and put this question to him, "Good master, what must I do to inherit eternal life?" Jesus said to him, "Why do you call me good? No one is good but God alone. You know the commandments: *You must not kill; You must not commit adultery; You must not steal; You must not bring false witness; You must not defraud; Honor your father and mother.*" And he said to him, "Master, I have kept all these from my earliest days." Jesus looked steadily at him and loved him, and he said, "There is one thing you lack. Go and sell everything you own and give the money to the poor, and you will have treasure in heaven; then come, follow me." But his face fell at these words and he went away sad, for he was a man of great wealth. (Mark 10:17-22)

Now allow yourself to daydream on the situation presented in the story. First picture the man approaching as Jesus is leaving on a journey. Then, as if you were a spectator, observe the events as they unfold. Watch, listen and stay attentive to Christ. Don't be distracted by the rich young ruler. And don't try to analyze the story or learn lessons from it. Just be present to Jesus and open to your own reactions. Put the book down now and spend four or five minutes trying this simple exercise.

﹆

I first began regularly meditating on the life of Christ in this way only in the past few years. After decades of Bible reading, I realized that my relationship with God was based more on what I believed than on what I experienced. I had lots of information about God but longed to deepen my personal knowing. Getting to know Jesus better seemed like the right place to start. It was.

The journey, however, has not been easy. I have trouble visualizing things, and my imagination is—at best—quite stunted. I often find that the details of my mental image of a scene are exclusively those suggested in the biblical account. I seem to have trouble letting the Spirit enrich the picture by adding other sensory details in the way he does for others. But after I get past my frustration and sense of failure, I realize that simply pondering the event—allowing myself to daydream on it—is sharing Jesus' experiences with him. I am, in fact, slowly moving into a new level of personal knowing of Jesus.

I also encounter the inevitable experience of wandering attention. You may have experienced this as well when you tried the brief meditation exercise above. If so, don't worry. Wandering thoughts are inevitable. As soon as you become aware of them, simply return your attention to the meditation. Drifting thoughts reflect the way God made our brains to follow pathways of associations, so don't allow yourself to get upset when this occurs.

Another struggle for me was the feeling that meditation was a waste of time. I wanted to judge it by what I got out of it. When I did, it often seemed to be a dreadfully inefficient spiritual practice. But productivity and efficiency miss the point. What God wants is simply our presence, even if it feels like a waste of potentially productive time. That is what friends do together—they waste time with each other. Simply being together is enough without expecting to "get something" from the interaction. It should be no different with God.

Spending time with Jesus in Gospel meditation has begun to put flesh on the God I have been seeking to know for so many years. As Jesus has begun to become more human and real to me, the invisible God of whom he is the image has become more accessible. Jesus bridges heaven and earth, the human and the divine. If he is so divine that we cannot meet him in his humanity, God remains wholly Other. But in Jesus, God is present. This is the truth of Immanuel—God with us.

There is no substitute for meditation on the life of Jesus if we seek to ground our God-knowing in the Gospels. Listening to sermons and reading the Bible provide information about Jesus, but this is not the same as a personal meeting of him in the events of his life. Meditation ought to be a part of the prayer life of every Christian who seriously seeks to genuinely know God. The Gospels provide wonderfully rich opportunities to meet Jesus, once we learn how to use them in this manner.

Gospel meditation is gazing on Christ. When Jesus compared himself to the bronze serpent that God told Moses to make for the children of Israel to gaze upon when they were dying of snakebites (John 3:14-15), one of the things he was saying was that gazing on Christ in trust and devotion allows the Spirit of God to take his life and make it ours.[5] God gave us Jesus as the Divine Image so that we could gaze upon him and thereby come to know God. This is why Gospel meditation holds such transformational power.

### MEETING GOD IN THE EVENTS OF LIFE

A second extremely rich resource for spending time with God is the discernment of Divine Presence in daily experience. Life, as Carolyn Gratton notes, keeps happening.[6] Changing life situations—some desirable and others definitely less so—provide important opportunities to better know both God and our self. Each gives us a chance to examine where God is in that experience and what gifts God is offering for our growth.

This second way of knowing God is not as different from the first as it might appear. Both involve meeting God in the concrete circumstances of life. Both therefore support the development of a practical, down-to-earth spirituality in which we encounter God in the mundane and familiar parts of regular life. Paul Stevens describes such a spirituality: "If God has come in the flesh, and if God keeps coming to us in our fleshly existence, then all of life is shot through with meaning. Earth is crammed with heaven, and heaven (when we finally get there) will be crammed with earth. Nothing wasted. Nothing lost. Nothing secular. Nothing absurd. . . . All are grist for the mill of a down-to-earth spirituality."[7]

The omnipresent God whose name is Immanuel is not distant but nearer to us than we can imagine. God is not alien to the circumstances of our lives but comes to us in them. Our challenge is to unmask the Divine in the natural and name the presence of God in our lives.[8]

A friend just wrote me, telling me of her despair and profound hopelessness in the face of the suffering of many people in her country. "But," she said, "I dare to hope that even in this despair I meet the Lord who weeps with me over those whose pain is so unimaginable and for whom hope is so dangerous." She was right. God is in her experience of despair, waiting for her to identify the Divine Presence and offering this as accompaniment on the often difficult journey of being human.

It is relatively easy to meet God in moments of joy or bliss. In these situations we correctly count ourselves blessed by God. The challenge is to believe that this is also true—and to know God's presence—in the midst of doubt, depression, anxiety, conflict or failure. But the God who is Immanuel is equally in those moments we would never choose as in those we would always gladly choose.

Richard Rohr reminds us that "we cannot attain the presence of God. We're already totally in the presence of God. What's absent is awareness."[9] This is the core of the spiritual journey—learning to discern the presence of God, to see what really is. But nothing is more dangerous than presuming that we already see when we do not.

The truth is that God is to be found in all things—even and most especially in the painful, tragic and unpleasant things. Jesus was the suffering Savior who knew every temptation and negative human experience that we could ever know. God's heart contains every conceivable human emotion. It contains us no matter what we experience. The omnipresent Christian God whose company cannot be evaded by going to hell, the depths of the sea or the heights of the heavens (Psalm 139:7-12) is a God who is present to us in every moment of our life.

Most of us learn to discern God's presence by first looking for it in the rearview mirror. That is the value of a prayerful review of the day—something I have elsewhere described as the daily examen.[10] Lucinda described her first experience of this as follows:

> After settling into my favorite chair and asking God to help me review the day I immediately thought of a troubling encounter with a colleague that morning. She poked her head in my office and asked about the visit she knew I had with my parents on the weekend. Although I talk with her nearly every day, I had never talked about my family, and suddenly I found myself embarrassed in doing so. There was nothing shameful to tell, but strangely, I found myself feeling as if I wanted to hide. I quickly ended the conversation and hadn't thought about it again until that moment.
>
> Asking Jesus to help me reflect on this was scary. I wasn't sure I wanted to know these feelings. They felt familiar— always avoided, but lurking at the edges of my experience. I told God that with his help I wanted to face them. I remembered other times when I had felt something similar. Previously I always ran from this as quickly as possible. This time I vowed to stay with it if God would help me.
>
> I'm still not sure I know where the feeling comes from or what it means. I have only reflected on one event in one day. But I feel I have taken an important step.

I wrote Lucinda back and asked if she had learned anything about God from this experience. She replied:

> Sitting with my shame in God's presence helped me see that God wasn't shocked by it. In fact, he seemed to know all about it. And he still accepted me! I became aware that whatever the shame was about, I did not need to hide from it, because God already knew about it. Sharing it with God allowed me to experience his love for a tender, vulnerable part of me.

Lucinda's experience demonstrates how knowledge of God and knowledge of self go hand in hand. Transformational knowing of God comes from meeting God in our depths, not in the abstraction of dusty theological propositions.

The goal of a prayerful review of recent life experiences is not self-analysis. The point is not to peel back the layers of the onion and find some problem or meaning. Instead the goal is simply increased awareness of God in the events of life and the depths of my being. It is attending to the God who is present. In general, "what" questions (such as, What was I feeling? What disturbed me about that comment? What exactly made me anxious?) are better than "why" questions (Why did I feel threatened? Why did that bother me?). And avoid making demands of yourself or God. Just accept whatever comes from each experience, each day.

## READY FOR DEEPER KNOWING OF GOD?

If the idea of Gospel meditation and prayerful review of recent experience stirs interest in you, consider committing yourself to fifteen minutes at the end of each day for the next week to do the following.

1. First, take your journal (or something on which you can write) and find a quiet place where you can sit undisturbed.

2. Select a Gospel account of one event in the life of Christ. After a brief prayer inviting God to allow you to imaginatively enter this experience and encounter Jesus, spend five minutes daydreaming on the passage.

3. After thanking God for the gift of time spent with Jesus, ask for help in reflecting on your day in order to better discern Divine Presence during it.

4. Allow the events of the day to replay before you. Accept whatever comes into focus, no matter how trivial it initially appears to be, as a gift from God. Ask for help to discern Divine Presence in the experience.

5. End your time by thanking God for gifts received during this process.

There is no simple formula for deep knowing of God. Vicki—who in my imagination has been sitting beside me as I wrote this chapter—has learned to avoid anything or anyone that suggests otherwise. You should do the same.

This chapter doesn't even begin to exhaust all the ways you can come to know God. But honest and prayerful reflection on the Gospels and daily experience provide a rich opportunity to meet God in ways that will change you. And as we have seen, it also allows you to meet yourself in deeper places.

# three

# First Steps Toward Knowing Yourself

Although we speak of certain people as being self-made, no one is truly their own creation. Personhood is not an accomplishment; it is a gift. As we shall see in chapter six, our true self—the self we are becoming in God—is something we receive from God. Any other identity is of our own making and is an illusion.

Knowing ourselves must therefore begin by knowing the self that is known by God. If God does not know us, we do not exist. And as noted by Merton (with his tongue firmly planted in his cheek), "to be unknown by God is altogether too much privacy!"[1]

The possibility of knowing yourself is grounded in the fact that your self is already known to God. Similarly, the possibility of your knowing God is grounded in the fact that God already knows you. J. I. Packer correctly captures the priority in all this knowing: "What matters supremely, therefore, is not, in the last analysis, the fact that I know God, but the larger fact which underlies it—the fact that *he knows me.*"[2] We are graven on the palms of God's hands and never out of the Divine mind. All our knowledge of God depends on God's sustained initiative in knowing us. We know God, because God first knew us, and continues to know us.

Genuine self-knowledge begins by looking at God and noticing how God is looking at us. Grounding our knowing of our self in God's knowing of us anchors us in reality. It also anchors us in God.

## KNOWING YOURSELF AS DEEPLY LOVED

The question is, how does God feel about you? What is God's knowing of you?

One young woman told me she feels afraid because she is sure God is mad at her. She thinks God is preoccupied with her sins and shortcomings and views her with anger and reproach. Is she right?

I also think of a friend who can no longer believe that God takes a personal interest in humans. As one among billions of people on the face of the earth, he suspects that he and the rest of us fail to register as individuals on God's consciousness. He tells me that he wishes he could believe God loves him but he cannot be persuaded that it is possible. Is he right?

I am convinced that God loves each and every one of us with depth, persistence and intensity beyond imagination. God doesn't simply like you. Nor does God simply have warm sentimental feelings toward you just because you were created in the Divine image. The truth is that God loves you with what Hannah Hurnard calls "a passionate absorbed interest."[3] God cannot help seeing you through eyes of love.

Even more remarkable, God's love for you has nothing to do with your behavior. Neither your faithlessness nor your unfaithfulness alters Divine love in the slightest degree. Like the father's love in the parable of the prodigal son, Divine love is absolutely unconditional, unlimited and unimaginably extravagant.

Christians affirm a foundation of identity that is absolutely unique in the marketplace of spiritualities. Whether we realize it or not, our being is grounded in God's love. The generative love of God was our origin. The embracing love of God sustains our existence. The inextinguishable love of God is the only hope for our fulfillment. Love is our identity and our calling, for we are children of Love. Created from love, of love and for love, our existence makes no sense apart from Divine love.

Neither knowing God nor knowing self can progress very far unless it begins with a knowledge of how deeply we are loved by God. Until we dare to believe that *nothing* can separate us from God's love—nothing that we could do or fail to do, nor anything that could be done by anyone else to us (Romans 8:31-39)—we remain in the elementary grades of the school of Christian spiritual transformation.[4]

In order for our knowing of God's love to be truly transformational, it must become the basis of our identity. Our identity is who we experience ourselves to be—the I each of us carries within. An identity grounded in God would mean that when we think of who we are, the first thing that would come to mind is our status as someone who is deeply loved by God.

With sadness I confess how seldom this is true for me. Although I have always wanted to avoid being defined by my professional role, when asked to introduce myself, I am likely to resort to the common social practice of trotting out vocational designations. But, even more telling, if my self-esteem is threatened and I feel my identity to be a bit vulnerable, my almost automatic first response is to think of accomplishments or present and future projects. What this tells me is that much more than I usually care to acknowledge, my identity is based on what I do, not who I am.

Christ presents a particularly poignant contrast to this. His identity was defined by his relationship to his Father. This was who he was. His whole life flowed out from this. What he did was not the basis of his identity but rather pointed to who he was: "The works my Father has given me to carry out, these same works of mine testify that the Father has sent me" (John 5:36).

At his baptism, Jesus had heard a Divine declaration of love for him as the Son with whom God was well pleased (Matthew 3:17). Jesus seemed to never doubt this. His relationship to the Father was the basis of how he experienced and understood himself. He was one with his Father in love—God being in him and he being in God (John 14:11). Nothing was more certain for him than the love of his Father, a love that he knew had existed from before the foundation of the world (John 17:24). Doing his Father's will grew out of this relationship of love that was the basis of his identity.

Even when Jesus felt that God had abandoned him in the Garden of Gethsemane, his confidence in the love of the Father was so great that he still desired God's will over his own. Jesus knew that he was loved whether or not he *felt* it. His identity was grounded in God.

But in case you find yourself thinking, *Of course God loves Jesus. After all, he was Jesus,* it might be helpful to recall that the Bible is full of other examples of the way knowing God's love transforms the self. For example, the Samaritan woman who met Jesus at the well (John 4:7-30), used to being an outcast to Jews, was astounded by how Jesus treated her. His approaching rather than avoiding her, talking to her and even asking for something from her must have surprised her greatly. And still after he put his finger on her moral failure, the expected did not happen. He did not condemn her! He did not even tell her to go and sin no more. Instead, after revealing her to herself, he revealed himself to her, disclosing his identity as the Messiah.

Revelation usually begins, as it did for this woman, by God's revealing us to ourselves. Only then does God reveal the Divine self to us.

Touched by perfect love, she would never be the same again. She had encountered the Lord.

Coming to know and trust God's love is a lifelong process. Making this knowledge the foundation of our identity—or better, allowing our identity to be re-formed around this most basic fact of our existence—will also never happen instantly. Both lie at the core of the spiritual transformation that is the intended outcome of Christ-following.

Every time I dare to meet God in the vulnerability of my sin and shame, this knowing is strengthened. Every time I fall back into a self-improvement mode and try to bring God my best self, it is weakened. I only know Divine unconditional, radical and reckless love for me when I dare to approach God just as I am. The more I have the courage to meet God in this place of weakness, the more I will know myself to be truly and deeply loved by God. And the more deeply I know this love, the easier it will be to trust it as Christ did—preferring God's will to my own.

❧

Set the book aside for a moment and reflect on your knowing of God's love. How much does this knowing form the foundation of your identity? In what ways do you experience Divine love? And how do you know it to be true even when you do not experience it?

If you do not like your answers to these questions—or if you feel stuck in this aspect of the journey—tell God how much you long to know perfect love. Pray that God will lead you to someone with whom you can share this desire, someone with the spiritual maturity to journey with you as you seek to know God's love experientially.

Moving truths such as "God loves me" from our head to our heart is often difficult. It is possible, but only as we journey with others. The God who is Divine community is known only in human community. Deep knowing of perfect love, just like deep knowing of ourselves, demands that we be in relationships of spiritual friendship.[5] No one should ever expect to make the journey alone. And the knowing of self and God described in these pages depends on being accompanied by others on our journey into the heart of God.

## KNOWING YOUR IGNORED PART-SELVES

Genuinely transformational knowing of self always involves encountering and embracing previously unwelcomed parts of self. While we tend to think of ourselves as a single, unified self, what we call "I" is really a family of many part-selves. That in itself is not a particular problem. The problem lies in the fact that many of these part-selves are unknown to us. Even though they are usually known to others, we remain blissfully oblivious of their existence.

To say that we are a family of many part-selves is not the same as saying that we play different roles. Most of us know what it is to be a friend, employee, church member, and possibly a parent or a spouse. Each of these roles is different, and most of us can move between them effortlessly. This is not the problem.

The problem is that there are important aspects of our experience that we ignore. Many of us, like the woman mentioned in chapter two, refuse to face our feelings of shame. They make us feel too vulnerable. So we pretend they do not exist and hope they will go away. Or it may be our broken and wounded self that we try to deny. When we do so, however, these unwanted parts of self do not go away. They simply go into hiding.

If, for example, I only know my strong, competent self and am never able to embrace my weak or insecure self, I am forced to live a lie. I must pretend that I *am* strong and competent, not simply that I *have* strong and competent parts or that under certain circumstances I *can be* strong and competent. Similarly, if I refuse to face my deceitful self I live an illusion regarding my own integrity. Or if I am unwilling to acknowledge my prideful self, I live an illusion of false modesty.

There is enormous value in naming and coming to know these excluded parts of self. My playful self, my cautious self, my exhibitionistic self, my pleasing self, my competitive self and many other faces of my self all are parts of me, whether I acknowledge their presence or not. Powerful conditioning in childhood encourages us to acknowledge only the most acceptable parts of our self. And parts of self that are not given a place at the family table become stronger, not weaker. Operating out of sight and beyond awareness, they have increasing influence on our behavior.

Christian spirituality involves acknowledging all our part-selves, exposing them to God's love and letting him weave them into the new person he is making. To do this, we must be willing to welcome these ignored parts as full members of the family of self, giving them space at the family table and slowly allowing them to be softened and healed by love and integrated into the whole person we are becoming.

## From Self to God

To illustrate this process of knowing self and embracing our unwelcome part-selves, as well as the way it can lead to a knowing of God, let me tell the story of someone I will call Judith.

I first met Judith as a student in a course I was teaching at St. Michael's University College, one of the affiliated Roman Catholic colleges of the University of Toronto. The course, Psychology and Christian Spirituality, was open to any of the fifty-five thousand undergraduate students at the university, and it was always interesting to see who signed up for it. Judith introduced herself after the first lecture, identifying herself as a Jew who was on the road to becoming a Christian.

Judith had been raised in a secular Jewish home. Being a Jew, she said, was a matter of ethnicity, not religion. The latter had held no interest for her until quite recently. What had been of interest was knowing herself. In addition to a major in psychology, she had been in psychoanalysis for several years and through this had come to meet herself in deep places. She told me of the courage she had developed as she learned to face the frightening parts of herself—her sexuality in particular. She also told me of the increased freedom to love others and genuinely be herself that had resulted. But what really captured my attention was her declaration that her work with an agnostic Jewish psychoanalyst had led her toward Christianity.

Judith's interest in God began as a result of her analyst's repeated encouragement to face truth. This, she said, was his therapeutic motto. As she learned to face the truth about herself, she became aware of spiritual longings that had long lain dormant and undetected. Her first step in responding to these was to explore Jewish spirituality by attending synagogue and beginning to read some of the Jewish mystics. After a while on this journey, she read something about the life of Teresa of Ávila, and this piqued her interest in Christianity. After reading Teresa's *Interior Castle*, she began to devour as much of the classic literature of Christian spirituality as she could find. This was the point at which she enrolled in my course.

Judith did in fact become a Christian. And as she began to know and love the God she had first encountered in the lives of the Christian saints, her knowing of herself deepened. Most striking was the way discovering God's acceptance of her in her totality aided the work she had been doing in psychoanalysis. Even her analyst commented on this fact. Encountering the frightening parts of herself in God's presence and noting God's embrace of all of her gave her the courage to slowly begin to undo her long-term repression of her sexuality. Bit by bit she dared bring her shameful and frightening part-selves into the circle of God's loving embrace, and bit by bit she came to know both herself and God more deeply.

Judith's story is not as unusual as it may seem. All humans are created spiritual beings with deep longings to find their identity in God. Those who honestly seek to know themselves will inevitably encounter these longings and face choices about how to respond to them. Deep knowing of self gives opportunity for deep knowing of God, just as deep knowing of God gives opportunity for deep knowing of self. It turns out just as John Calvin said it would be.

## SELF-ACCEPTANCE AND SELF-KNOWING

Allowing God to accept me just as I am helps me accept myself in the same way. This is essential for genuine spiritual transformation.

Self-acceptance and self-knowing are deeply interconnected. To truly know something about yourself, you must accept it. Even things about yourself that you most deeply want to change must first be accepted—even embraced. Self-transformation is always preceded by self-acceptance. And the self that you must accept is the self that you actually and truly are—*before you start your self-improvement projects!*

Any hope that you can know yourself without accepting the things about you that you wish were not true is an illusion. Reality must be embraced before it can be changed. Our knowing of ourselves will remain superficial until we are willing to accept ourselves as God accepts us—fully and unconditionally, just as we are.

God's acceptance of us as we are is not in any way in conflict with Divine longing for our wholeness. Nor is our acceptance of our self. But until we are prepared to accept the self we actually are, we block God's transforming work of making us into our true self that is hidden in God. We must befriend the self we seek to know. We must receive it with hospitality, not hostility. No one—not even your own self—can be known apart from such a welcome.

Let me illustrate this by returning to the story of Peter. It is highly unlikely that his betrayal of Christ was his first encounter with the fear that must have been behind this act. Almost certainly he had previously found himself in situations when fear made him back away from an action he wanted to take. Unless he had totally repressed these experiences, he would be able to recall them. However, possessing such information about himself would not have been the same as truly knowing himself.

The difference lies in self-acceptance. Until we are willing to accept the unpleasant truths of our existence, we rationalize or deny responsibility for our behavior. Thus, refusing to face and accept his cowardice and fear, Peter may, for example, have explained away cowardly acts by focusing on the circumstances. He could have followed the same strategy after his denial of Jesus. Perhaps that is what Jesus anticipated and sought to circumvent by his public prediction of Peter's denial. But the choice of whether to accept reality and himself was Peter's and his alone.

If God loves and accepts you as a sinner, how can you do less? You can never be other than who you are until you are willing to embrace the reality of who you are. Only then can you truly become who you are most deeply called to be.

Some Christians become quite upset at the suggestion that self-acceptance must precede transformation. They argue that self-acceptance is the exact opposite of what we are supposed to do to the parts of self that do not honor God. What we are supposed to do, they say, is crucify them, not embrace them.

Scriptures seem clear enough about the importance of crucifying our sin nature (Romans 8:13). But attempts to eliminate things that we find in our self that we do not first accept as part of us rely on denial, not crucifixion. Crucifixion should be directed toward our sin nature. And we must first accept it as *our* nature, not simply *human* nature. Only after we genuinely know and accept everything we find within our self can we begin to develop the discernment to know what should be crucified and what should be embraced as an important part of self.

Freud noted that things about ourselves that we refuse to acknowledge are given increased power and influence by our failure to accept them. It is that which we avoid, he asserted, that will most tyrannize us. In this he was absolutely right. Self-acceptance does not increase the power of things that ultimately need to be eliminated. Rather, it weakens them. It does so because it robs them of the power that they develop when they operate outside of awareness and outside the embrace of self-acceptance.

Before we can surrender ourselves we must become ourselves, for no one can give up what he or she does not first possess.[6] Jesus puts it this way: "If you're content with simply being yourself, you will become more than yourself" (Luke 18:14 *The Message*). Before we can become our self we must accept our self, just as we are. Self-acceptance always precedes genuine self-surrender and self-transformation.

## SEARCHING FOR THE SPIRITUAL KEY

Nasrudin[7]—the protagonist of many Middle Eastern, Greek and Russian folktales—was approaching the door of his house one night when he suddenly realized he had lost his key. He tried to look around for it, but the night was so dark he could hardly see the ground. So he got down on his hands and knees and examined the ground where he was standing. But it was still too dark to see anything. Moving back toward a streetlamp, he again got down and began a meticulous examination of the area.

A friend came by and, noticing him, asked what he was doing. Nasrudin replied, "I lost my key and am looking for it." So the friend too got down on his hands and knees and began to search.

After a while the friend asked, "Do you remember where you might have lost the key?"

"Certainly," answered Nasrudin. "I lost it in my house."

"Then why are you looking for it out here?"

"Because," answered Nasrudin, "the light is so much better here."

We are all much more like Nasrudin than we like to acknowledge. We search for a missing spiritual key, but we tend to look for it outside of ourselves where it seems easiest to search. But the key is inside, in the dark.

Jesus said, "When you pray, go to your private room and, when you have shut your door, pray to your Father who is in that secret place" (Matthew 6:6). The secret place where we encounter God in a truly transformational way is in our inner self. Prayer is meeting God in the darkness and solitude of that secret place. Nothing less than such an encounter with God in the depths of our soul will provide access to the deep knowing of both God and self that is our true home.

What makes this encounter possible is looking at God looking at us. As we see how deeply loved we are by God—in our depths, complexity, totality and sinfulness—we dare to allow God more complete access to the dark parts of our soul that most need transformation. And God precedes us on this journey, waiting to meet us in the depths of our self.

# four

# Knowing Yourself as You Really Are

Knowing the depths of God's personal love for each of us as individuals is the foundation of all genuine self-knowledge. But there is yet more to be learned from reflecting on how God knows us.

The self that God persistently loves is not my prettied-up pretend self but my actual self—the real me. But, master of delusion that I am, I have trouble penetrating my web of self-deceptions and knowing this real me. I continually confuse it with some ideal self that I wish I were.

The roots of our pretend self lie in our childhood discovery that we can secure love by presenting ourselves in the most flattering light. A little girl hides her hatred of her brother because she knows that she should love him. This lack of integrity is then reinforced by her parents, who commend her loving behavior. A young boy denies his resentment after he fails to get something he desires. In so doing, he takes a step toward a loss of awareness of what he is really feeling. In short, we learn to fake it, appearing as we think important others want us to be and ignoring the evidence to the contrary.

This may all seem quite innocent. However, it sheds its innocence when we lose touch with our actual experience, because this always involves a diminishment of our grounding in reality.

Thomas Merton warns, "There is no greater disaster in the spiritual life than to be immersed in unreality, for life is maintained and nourished in us by our vital relation with reality."[1] The truly spiritual life is not an escape from reality but a total commitment to it.

Most of us are quite willing to embrace reality when it fits with how we see ourselves and the world, and when it is not overly unpleasant. However, when our life experiences confront us with things about ourselves that we are unwilling to accept, we call on psychological defense mechanisms to help maintain a sense of safety and stability. While these unconscious strategies help with short-term coping, they block long-term growth. This is because they distort reality. Ultimately, their function is to protect us from unpleasant truth.

The human capacity for self-deception is astounding. This is taught by Scripture (Jeremiah 17:9) and confirmed by psychology. Some people are highly skilled in deceiving others. However, their duplicity pales in comparison with the endlessly creative ways in which each and every one of us deceives our self.

Self-deception occurs automatically. This is part of what psychologists mean when they say that the defense mechanisms operate in the unconscious. It is also part of what theologians mean when they speak of original sin. We don't really have to choose self-deception. It is—to use contemporary computer jargon—the default option.

We are usually quite adept at identifying self-deception in others. In someone else we easily see a rigid embrace of niceness at the expense of any acknowledgment of anger or resentment. This is the defense mechanism of *reaction formation:* some unacceptable feeling or impulse is eliminated from awareness by our expression of its opposite. In another person we identify a *rationalization* when they give a good reason for their behavior but not the real reason. In yet someone else, a simple *denial* of feelings that are obviously present illustrates the most basic form of self-deception that exists.

Recognizing these same things in ourselves is much more difficult. The penetration of our delusions is enormously challenging. It requires a relentless commitment to truth and a deep sense of freedom from fear of rejection. Nothing facilitates this like the knowledge of being deeply loved.

Spiritual transformation involves the purification of sight. Jesus said that if our eye is healthy, our whole body will be full of light (Luke 11:34). We have to learn to see—and accept—what is really there. Stripping away our illusions is part of this process, as it reorients us toward reality. To see God as God is—not as who we want God to be—requires that we see our self as we actually are. For the same cloud of illusions obscures our view of both God and ourselves.

## KNOWING YOURSELF AS A SINNER

Knowing ourselves as we really are inevitably brings us up against what the Bible calls sin. It doesn't take much self-awareness to recognize that there are some very basic things about us that are not as they should be. Let me speak for myself. I do things I do not want to do and seem incapable of doing other things that I wish to do. I seem to be programmed for selfishness and egocentricity, not love. If I am honest, I must admit that my motivation is never as pure or noble as I wish it to appear. My ability to realize my potential as a person made in God's image seems to be sabotaged by some inner agenda over which I have no control. This is an important part of what it means to be a sinner.

Daily experience impresses upon me the painful fact that my heart has listened to the serpent instead of God. As James Finley says with brutal honesty, "There is something in me that puts on fig leaves of concealment, kills my brother, builds towers of confusion, and brings cosmic chaos upon the earth. There is something in me that loves darkness rather than light, that rejects God and thereby rejects my own deepest reality as a human person made in the image and likeness of God."[2]

Some Christians base their identity on being a sinner. I think they have it wrong—or only half right. You are not simply a sinner; you are a deeply loved sinner. And there is all the difference in the world between the two.

Sin is a corollary to our primary status as greatly loved children of God. First we were loved into being, created in the good and sinless image of our Creator God. And although sin damaged that which had been utterly good, it allowed us to discover that God's love is directed toward us just as we are, as sinners. The sequence is important. We must never confuse the secondary fact with the primary truth.

Real knowing of ourselves can only occur after we are convinced that we are deeply loved precisely as we are. The fact that God loves and knows us as sinners makes it possible for us to know and love our self as sinner. It all starts with knowing God's love.

For it to be meaningful, knowing ourselves as sinners must involve more than knowing that we commit certain sins. Sin is more basic than what we do. Sin is who we are. In this regard we could say that sin is fundamentally a matter of ontology (being), not simply morality. To be a human is to be a sinner. It is to be broken, damaged goods that carry within our deepest self a fundamental, fatal flaw—a flaw that masks our original creation goodness and infects our very being.

If all we know about ourselves is the specific sins we commit, our self-understanding remains superficial. Focusing on sins leads to what Dallas Willard describes as the gospel of sin management[3]—a resolve to avoid sin and strategies to deal with guilt when this inevitably proves unsuccessful. But Christian spiritual transformation is much more radical than sin avoidance. And the knowing of self that is required for such transformation is much deeper.

Knowing our sinfulness becomes most helpful when we get behind sins to our core sin tendencies. Now we shift our focus from behavior to the heart.

## GETTING BEHIND SINS TO SIN

Stuart was a pastor who came to me for psychotherapy for a sexual addiction. He felt tremendously guilty about his longstanding use of pornography but also felt totally helpless to change it. After years of confessing his sin, praying for help and then falling back into old habits, he had concluded that he must leave the ministry. His bishop had encouraged him to see me before making a final decision. In desperation, and with very little hope, he agreed.

Our work together took Stuart down a dark and difficult path of self-understanding. Behind the sexual addiction we discovered a longing for intimacy, not a reservoir of lust. His marriage provided as much genuine intimacy as he could tolerate, but in fantasy he sought ways of experiencing intimacy that did not make the demands on him of a real relationship. More important, however, we discovered a high degree of resentment and a strong sense of entitlement. As we explored this, he became aware of a feeling that he deserved something better than he was experiencing. It was this that ultimately led us to his core sin tendency—pride.

At root, Stuart was deeply bitter that no one recognized how special he was. As we explored this feeling, he was able to trace it back to childhood. He had felt overlooked in his large family of six siblings. He had been the responsible one who took care of everyone else, but no one seemed to appreciate him for this. He had also been the one with the most marked accomplishments, but again, no one seemed to take any special note of this fact.

Stuart had learned to cover his resentment over his unnoticed specialness with a mask of false humility. But beneath this lay a smoldering fire of bitterness. Pride suggested that he deserved special treatment. When he didn't get this, he withdrew in hurt and anger. This, in turn, led to a sense of being cut off and deprived of intimacy. And this was behind his attraction to pornography.

Discovering that he longed for intimacy, not simply sexual gratification, was not in itself transformational for Stuart. However, accepting the emotionally needy little boy who longed for and yet feared loving embrace was. Confronting the depths of his pride and sense of entitlement was enormously difficult. But Stuart began to find freedom only when he accepted himself as he found himself to be accepted by God—in the midst of his sin.

Stuart illustrates how genuine acceptance brings clarity and discernment about the nature of our problems. For years he had sought to crucify his sexual desires, being convinced that they were the core of his problem. But rather than crucifying his sexuality, he needed to embrace it, hospitably receiving this very important part of himself and thus allowing it to be integrated within the fabric of the total self. He needed to welcome back this wayward part of self that had become wild and untamed from so many years in exile. Treated like the enemy, his sexuality had begun to function like the enemy. But once he accepted that he was not a sexual monster, just a normal male with normal sexual needs, his sexual needs seemed to recede in strength and prominence.

Discovering our core sin tendencies is helpful because it lets us deal with our problems at their root. But even more than this, it is helpful because discovery of our core sin tendencies will inevitably fill us with such despair and hopelessness that we will have no option but to turn to God. Spiritual transformation does not result from fixing our problems. It results from turning to God in the midst of them and meeting God just as we are. Turning to God is the core of prayer. Turning to God in our sin and shame is the heart of spiritual transformation.

The most important part of my work with Stuart was helping him feel free enough from judgment to risk honesty and awareness. Some of his discoveries about himself made him immediately feel hopeful. He felt that way as he began to understand the nonsexual nature of his addiction to pornography. Seeing it in a completely new light gave him new optimism as it suggested a new way to approach what had become an intractable problem. But other discoveries—particularly his new awareness of his sense of entitlement and the core of pride—left him feeling utterly overwhelmed, humiliated and hopeless. These things seemed to come from a place so deep within himself that he despaired of ever being able to do anything to fix them.

This insight was truly a gift. For it allowed him to meet God where God was already waiting to meet him—in the core of his brokenness and sin.

## An Ancient Aid to Deep Knowing of Our Sin

One tool that many people have found helpful in identifying basic sin tendencies is an ancient approach to understanding personality called the Enneagram[4] (pronounced "any-a-gram"). Unlike classifications of personality that are based on traits,[5] the organizing principle of the Enneagram is deeper and less attractive. It zeroes in on the fatal flaw, or basic sin, of each of nine personality types. No one should work with the Enneagram if what they seek is flattery. But no one should fail to do so if what they seek is deep knowing of self.

Our sinfulness is never simply reducible to one temptation. But the assumption behind the Enneagram is that underlying everything we do is one major temptation that is particular to us. And until we see it for what it is, we will inevitably give in to this temptation and live in bondage to it.

The core sins identified by the Enneagram are each associated with a core need.[6] The needs are basic human needs, such as a need for love, for security or for perfection. The sin consists in making these something of ultimate value—that is, making them into God.

- Ones need to be perfect and, discovering that neither they nor anything else in their world is perfect, are tempted by self-righteous anger. A good biblical example of this type is Paul.

- Twos need to be loved and needed, and their competence in making this happen sets them up for pride. Martha is a good biblical example of a Two.

- Threes need to be successful and are tempted to deceit, as they do whatever they have to do to avoid failure and appear in the best possible light. Jacob illustrates this type.

- Fours need to be special and are tempted toward envy, escapist fantasy and a compromise of authenticity. Joseph, the Old Testament patriarch, illustrates this type.

- Fives need knowledge, long for fulfillment, and are tempted by greed, stinginess and critical detachment. Thomas, the so-called doubting disciple, fits this pattern.

- Sixes need security and are tempted by fear, self-doubt and cowardice. Timothy is a good example of a Six.

- Sevens need to avoid pain and are tempted by gluttony and intemperance. Solomon is a biblical example of this type.

- Eights need power, self-reliance and opportunities to be against something and are tempted by lust, arrogance and the desire to possess and control others. King Saul is a good illustration of an Eight.

- Nines need to maintain emotional peace and avoid initiative and are tempted by laziness, comfortable illusions and being overly accommodating. Jonah illustrates this type.

I first discovered the Enneagram in 1988, during a period of some intense personal spiritual work. As often happens, the first type I identified as I sought to find myself within the system was wrong.[7] Unable to face deeper truths about myself, I identified with several superficial traits that were true of me—but not my deepest truth.

In the language of the Enneagram, I first thought I was a Five. The core sin of this type is greed, and I was able to see how, despite massive denial of this, I was in fact significantly motivated by greed. Many aspects of the personality style of Fives also fit quite well for me. These are people who tend to live in their head, observing life with detachment, objectivity and insight. With a voracious hunger for knowledge, their quest to understand the world and themselves is relentless. However, at times it keeps them from both intimacy with others and genuine and deep knowing of themselves. All this fits me. But by identifying with this type I was also protecting myself from a more painful encounter with my deepest sin tendencies.

Another type where I felt a good fit was a One. At this point in my life I was just beginning to understand and face my anger, and anger is the root sin of Ones. I could also identify with the core temptation to perfection and to doing the right thing for the wrong reason. Clearly there was some of the moralist in me, even if I was working hard to keep it under control. And I could identify with the tendency to become overly serious, dutiful and responsible. It seemed like a relatively good fit.

I also felt I saw a good deal of myself in the Two—people whose

root sin is pride and whose core temptation is to flattery and help-
fulness that is ultimately more self-serving than they recognize.
Needing others to like them, Twos are tempted to manipulate
others into needing them in some way or another. In general, they
control others by pleasing them. Many of these things seemed like
a reasonably good fit for me.

But although we all fit all nine types to some extent or another,
"reasonably good fits" always mean that you have not yet been able
to truly face the depths of your illusions and basic sin. Continued
prayerful reflection on what I was learning about myself from the
Enneagram slowly suggested that where I really fit was with Type
Three. As is always the case when one finds one's true type within
the Enneagram, this was initially accompanied by a horrifying
sense of humiliation. How could I dare name my basic sin as
deceit? How willing I suddenly was to own any of the other eight
basic sins! How profoundly exposed I suddenly felt!

Threes are not necessarily liars. It is simply that out of our profound fear of failure we tend to be good at putting the best possible
spin on things. Consequently we are never quite as healthy, competent, successful or whatever else we value as we appear. This is
the core of our deception. We also worship at the shrine of efficiency, and we usually do pretty well at measuring up against this
rather arbitrary self-established criterion of success. Appearances
count for Threes. We don't so much tell lies as we tend to live them.

Ouch! I knew I had found my type—my basic sin pattern.

The truth is that none of these types is worse or more sinful
than another. And none is more beyond redemption than another. While our basic personality type and core sinful temptation appears to remain constant over a lifetime, there is no
question that we can move toward greater freedom and wholeness
within the framework of who we are. This is the process of spiritual transformation.

Spiritual transformation, not self-knowledge, is the goal of Christian spirituality. With God's help we need to break through our illusions and see ourselves as we truly are in relation to God.

A complete knowing of our self in relation to God includes knowing three things: our self as deeply loved (dealt with in chapter three), our self as deeply sinful (the focus of this chapter), and our self as in a process of being redeemed and restored (which will be explored in chapter six). Facing these deep truths about ourselves makes it possible for us to accept and know ourselves as we are accepted and known by God.

## Prayerful Reflection

Genuinely knowing your self as you are known by God can be quite frightening. But if God knows you and still loves you deeply, there is hope that you can do the same! Genuine self-knowledge is available to all who (1) genuinely desire it, (2) are willing to prayerfully reflect on their experience and (3) have the courage to meet themselves and God in solitude.

If your self-knowledge is limited, prayerfully reflect on which of these three prerequisites is most deficient. If you hunger to know yourself more deeply, continue the daily prayer review suggested in chapter two. Also, watch for times when you can be alone with yourself and God. Often these times are already in the rhythm of your week but are filled with distractions to protect you from solitude. Some people have music on whenever they are alone. Others turn to their computer, television or their phone in ways that serve the same soul-numbing purposes. The possibilities for avoiding solitude are endless.

After prayerful reflection to identify the things you use to avoid solitude, covenant with God and yourself to set aside some time to simply be still with God in the depths of yourself. Don't give yourself any agenda for this time other than sitting with God in silence.

Begin with a simple prayer asking God to help you be still. Don't feel you need to fill your time with words or thoughts; just remain still and believe that you are in God's presence whether you sense it or not.

At the end of the time—not during it—write your experience in your journal. Note your thoughts, reactions and feelings and then give them up to God. The point is not analysis but identification and release. Note them for what they are and then give them to God. Self-knowledge is God's gift, not the result of your introspection. Remember, this is not self-therapy. It is spending time with God and allowing God to meet you and help you know yourself as you are known.

There is no substitute for meeting God in your depths if you really desire this knowing. Praying that you might see your self as God sees you takes courage. But if done with the deep assurance that the self you seek to know is already known and deeply loved by God, it is absolutely possible. And remember, it is in the depths of your self that God waits to meet you with transforming love.

# five

# Unmasking Your False Self

The ideal of authenticity is something like the ideal of perfection. All of us have some idea of what we are talking about without ever having had any direct personal experience of it.

What we do know from personal experience is how to scramble after what we think is our best shot at personal fulfillment. We all seek a way of being that will lead to happiness. The reality is, however, that not all routes are equally authentic. If there is a way of being that is true to my deepest self, then there are also many other ways that are false.

Everything that is false about us arises from our belief that our deepest happiness will come from living life our way, not God's way. Although we may say we want to trust God and surrender to his will, deep down we doubt that God is really capable of securing our happiness.

## PERSONAL STYLE

Early on in life most of us learn to take care of our own needs and satisfactions. We develop what Thomas Keating calls a personal emotional program.[1] This is our plan for coping with life and achieving happiness. It is our best guess about what we need to do in order to feel good about our self. It is our strategy for meeting our basic needs for love, survival, power and control.

Our basic style is often built around the things that were reinforced for us as children. It usually starts with the things we do well. Over time our repertoire of competencies grows, and we learn to live in a way that we think will work for us. This becomes "our way," or what we simply think of as who we are.

The problem is not that we do certain things well and have competencies and qualities that make us special. The problem lies in the inordinate investment that we place in this image and way of being.

At the core of the false self is a desire to preserve an image of our self and a way of relating to the world. This is our personal style—how we think of ourselves and how we want others to see us and think of us. I may have an image of myself as rational and careful. This will be at the core of my basic style. Alternately, my most prized trait might be my fitness, my intelligence or my sense of humor. Or it could be that my investment is in an image of someone who is loving, artistic, unpredictable, creative, fashionable, absent-minded, serious, spiritual or impulsive. Typically the trait that we prize is in fact part of who we are. But the truth always is that this trait is simply one among many. We live a lie when we make it the sum of our being.

Our false self is built on an inordinate attachment to an image of our self that we think makes us special. The problem is the attachment, not having qualities that make us unique. Richard Rohr suggests that the basic question we must ask is whether we are prepared to be other than our image of our self.[2] If not, we will live in bondage to our false self.

As an example of this life of bondage to a false self, consider Saul before his conversion and new identity as Paul. Ambitious, fanatically zealous and homicidally ruthless, Saul was the terror of first-century Christians. The Acts of the Apostles describes him as working for the total destruction of the church, going house to house arresting followers of Christ and sending them to prison or execution (Acts 8:1-3).

Saul's falsity is seen most clearly in the light of what was true in Paul. The persistence of Saul's hatred pointed to a life that was badly out of alignment, but what exactly was wrong? In retrospect I would suggest that he was consumed by personal ambition.

Saul was making a name for himself. He wanted to be known as the one who single-handedly saved Judaism from the heresy of Christianity. What changed when he met Christ on the Damascus Road was that his prodigious talents and extraordinary level of passion were redirected away from the kingdom of self to the kingdom of God. In this redirection he found freedom from the tyranny of his private ambition. He found his true self.

No longer driven by hatred, he was now compelled by love. His life as Paul showed much of the same dogged determination that was seen in his life as Saul. But now it was not his ambition to make his mark and do it his way that propelled him forward. Instead it was his longing to reach what he described as the mark of the high calling of God in Christ Jesus (Philippians 3:14 KJV).

## The Challenge of Authenticity

Something else that we know from experience is how to hide and how to pretend. At some point in childhood we all make the powerful discovery that we can manipulate the truth about ourselves. Initially it often takes the form of a simple lie—frequently a denial of having done something. But of more importance to the development of the false self is the discovery that our ability to hide isn't limited to what we say or don't say. We learn to pretend. We discover the art of packaging our self.

We learn that even if we feel afraid, we can appear to be brave.

We also learn to cloak hate with apparent love, anger with apparent calm, and indifference with apparent sympathy. In short, we learn how to present our self in the best possible light—a light designed to create a favorable impression and maintain our self-esteem.

While this might seem quite benign, the dark side of pretending is that what begins as a role becomes an identity. Initially the masks we adopt reflect how we want others to see us. Over time, however, they come to reflect how we want to see our self. But by this point we have thoroughly confused the mask and our actual experience. Our masks have become our reality, and we have become our lies. In short, we have lost authenticity and adopted an identity based on illusion. We have become a house of smoke and mirrors.

Few things are more difficult to discern and dismantle than our most cherished illusions. And none of our illusions are harder to identify than those that lie at the heart of our false self. The false self is like the air we breathe. We have become so accustomed to its presence that we are no longer aware of it. It is as elusive as the wind, seeming to disappear when the light of attention is shined in its direction.

The only hope for unmasking the falsity that resides at the core of our being is a radical encounter with truth. Nothing other than truth is strong enough to dispel illusion. And only the Spirit of Truth can save us from the consequences of having listened to the serpent rather than God.

## LISTENING TO THE SERPENT

The Genesis account of the temptation of Adam and Eve helps us understand how we become the lies we choose to believe. The story tells of a serpent that, knowing our first parents wanted to be like God, offered them a way to achieve this. Their desire to be like God was not in itself the problem. For God had created them in the Divine image and wanted them to be like God. However, God's gift of likeness was quite different from that offered by the deceiver.

The core of the lie that Adam and Eve believed was that they could be like God without God. But without God the most we can ever do is make ourselves into a god. The truth is that we cannot be like God by means of a spiritual coup of Divine authority and sovereignty. James Finley puts it this way:

> Any expression of self-proclaimed likeness to God is forbidden us, not because it breaks some law arbitrarily decreed by God, but because such an action is tantamount to a fundamental, death-dealing, ontological lie. We are not God. We are not our own origin, nor are we our own ultimate fulfillment. To claim to be so is a suicidal act that wounds our faith relationship with the living God and replaces it with a futile faith in a self that can never exist.[3]

Paradoxically, Adam and Eve got what they wanted—to be like God without God, likeness that was based on independence rather than surrender. This is why we must be very careful about what we desire. We might just get it!

However, what we get when we choose a way of being that is separate from God is the life of the lie. It is a lie because the autonomy that it promises is an illusion. We do not become free of God by a disregard of Divine will. Instead, by such disregard we forge the chains of our bondage.

What we get when we choose a way of being that is separate from God is the life of the false self. What Saul got when he chose his way over God's way was a self whose significance depended on accomplishments of heroic proportions—the destruction of the church. What Stuart (whose story I told in chapter four) got was an illusory sense of specialness based on the gratifications of pornography.

The false self is the tragic result of trying to steal something from God that we did not have to steal. Had we dared to trust

God's goodness, we would have discovered that everything we could ever most deeply long for would be ours in God. Trying to gain more than the everything God offers, we end up with less than nothing. Rejecting God, we end up with a nest of lies and illusions. Displacing God, we become a god unto our self. We become a false self.

## COPING WITH NAKEDNESS

With the self that is created in God's likeness rejected, our false self is the self we develop in our own likeness. This is the person we would like to be—a person of our own creation, the person we would create if we were God. But such a person cannot exist, because he or she is an illusion.

Basing identity on an illusion has profound consequences. Sensing its fundamental unreality, the false self wraps itself in experience—experiences of power, pleasure and honor. Intuiting that it is but a shadow, it seeks to convince itself of its reality by equating itself with what it does and achieves. Basil Pennington suggests that the core of the false self is the belief that my value depends on what I have, what I can do and what others think of me.[4] Thomas Merton describes this as "winding experiences around myself . . . like bandages in order to make myself perceptible to myself and to the world, as if I were an invisible body that could only become visible when something visible covered its surface."[5]

Because it is hollow at the core, the life of a false self is a life of excessive attachments. Seeking to avoid implosion and nonbeing, the false self grasps for anything that appears to have substance and then clings to these things with the tenacity of a drowning man clutching a life ring. One person might cling to his possessions, accomplishments or space. Another may cling to her dreams, memories or friendships. Any of these things can be either a blessing or a curse. They are a blessing when they are held in open hands of gratitude. They become a curse when they are grasped in clenched fists of entitlement and viewed as "me" or "mine."

Saul clung to his zeal and force of will. Sounding like the prototypical Enneagram Type One that he was, after his conversion he described this as his desire to attain perfection by the strength of his efforts (Philippians 3:6-9). What a relief it must have been for him to replace the perfection he had sought through hard work with "the perfection that comes through faith in Christ, and is from God" (Philippians 3:9).

We think of our attachments as anchors of well-being. We feel good when we are surrounded by what seem like innocent indulgences and think they secure a state of pleasure that would not be ours without them. In reality, however, they sabotage our happiness and are hazardous to both our spiritual health and our psychological health.

Attachments undermine our freedom, making our contentment and joy dependent on their presence. If my "innocent indulgence" is being surrounded by the latest high-tech gadgetry, I feel good when I get a new toy and not good when I see a newer version on the market and am unable to get it. An attachment to style, fashion and good taste operates the same way, making my happiness dependent on external things. Attachments imprison us in falsity as we follow the flickering sirens of desire.

Spiritually, attachments serve as idols: we invest in objects and experiences that should be invested only in God. Anything that is grasped is afforded value beyond actual worth, value that is ultimately stolen from God.

Ultimately, attachments are ways of coping with the feelings of vulnerability, shame and inadequacy that lie at the core of our false ways of being. Like Adam and Eve, our first response to our awareness of nakedness is to grab whatever is closest and quickly cover our nakedness. We hide behind the fig leaves of our false self. This is the way we package our self to escape the painful awareness of our nakedness.

The problem with the false self is that it works. It helps us forget that we are naked. Before long, we are no longer aware of the underlying vulnerability and become comfortable once again.

But God wants something better than fig leaves for us. God wants us to be aware of our helplessness so we can know that we need Divine help. God's deepest desire for us is to replace our fig leaves with garments of durability and beauty (Genesis 3:21). Yet we cling to our fig-leaf false self. We believe that we know how to take care of our needs better than God.

## Recognizing Your False Self

While other people's excessive attachments and personal falsity often seem glaringly apparent, it is never easy to know the lies of our own life. There are, however, some trustworthy clues if we dare to be honest enough to face them.

One of these is defensiveness. Because of its fundamental unreality, the false self needs constant bolstering. Touchiness dependably points us to false ways of being. And the more prickly a person you are, the more you are investing in the defense of a false self.

Some people bristle easily if they are not taken seriously, thus betraying a need for others to see the self-importance that is so obvious to them. Others take themselves too seriously, perhaps being unable to laugh at themselves. Both reactions suggest ego inflation. Others have learned to mask these outward displays of defensiveness, but inner reactions of annoyance or irritation still point toward the presence of a false self.

I have always disliked being called Dave. Sometimes I correct people who do so. More often I simply remind myself how trivial the matter is and attempt to ignore my irritation. The obvious question, though, is why I am making such a big deal out of one consonant at the end of a name!

The answer points back to the core of my false self. David—I confess—seems to fit better with the image of seriousness I want to project. Dave seems too common and ordinary, perhaps too familiar. In the puffed-up state of self-importance associated with my false self, I want to be unique and I want to be important. I don't want to be content with ordinary.

That's how the false self works. Its touchiness is predictable. Pettiness is one of its most stable characteristics. The things that bother us most about others—our pet peeves—also point toward falsity in our own self. The speck that bothers me in the life of someone else is almost always the log in my own eye (Matthew 7:3).

If laziness in others is what really bothers me, there is a good chance that discipline and performance form a core part of the false self that I embrace with tenacity. If it is playfulness and spontaneity in others that I find most annoying, then seriousness may be a central part of the self I protect and seek to project. If it is moral disregard that is particularly irritating in others, my false self is probably built around moral rectitude and self-righteousness. And if emotionality in others is what I most despise, emotional control is probably central to the script I have chosen to live.

Another clue to the nature of our false self is the pattern of our compulsions. Everyone tends to be compulsive about something, and for most of us it is what we think we most need. One person may compulsively pursue success or esteem, while another may invest the same energy in avoiding pain or emotional unpleasantness. There is nothing wrong with any of these things. The problem with compulsions is that they represent excessive attachments. They often involve a good that is elevated to the status of the supreme good by the disproportionate importance we attach to it.

Perfection may be desirable if welcomed as God's work in us, but not as an outcome of the relentless effort people like Saul tend to expend to produce it. Love is certainly also an unquestionable good, but the compulsive effort to always be loving that characterizes others reflects a denial of their humanity and always comes at the expense of authenticity. Similarly, success, beauty, knowledge, security, pleasure, self-reliance and contentment are all good things, but not the supreme good that we make them when we invest in them inordinately.

The most basic function of our compulsions is to help us preserve our false self. But maintaining this illusion is the source of all our unhappiness. As Basil Pennington observes, unhappiness is always a result of "not being able to do something I want to do, have something I want to have, or concern about what others will think of me."[6] This brings us back to the core of the false self—placing my value in what I have, what I can do and what others think of me.

## THE ILLUSION OF THE FALSE SELF

Perhaps an illustration will help clarify these false ways of being. While I would rather tell someone else's story, my own is the one I know best.

The root of my false self was the childhood discovery that by being a good boy I could earn love. Of course, learning how to interpret "good" took some time. A false self is never established overnight! However, over time the interaction of the dynamics of my family and of my personality suggested ways of wrapping my naked and vulnerable self with successive layers of accomplishment to secure love.

The problem was that these strategies worked. The more I accomplished, the more people seemed to like me. Consequently, I became better and better at being the little performing boy that I thought people would like. This gave me some distance from the abyss of feeling like a nobody. Even more important, it gave me a way of being not just a somebody, but somebody special. Tragically, however, it kept me from discovering just how likable I was without any effort to look good. And it set me up on a treadmill of performance.

Securing love by generating accomplishments leaves one dependent on the potentially fickle response of others. As I look back, it seems I put a spin on this as I shifted from seeking love to seeking respect, something that I unconsciously realized made the supply of love even more secure. While love is freely given, respect is earned.

My longstanding investment in being respected has been an attempt to control my environment and guarantee the sense of specialness to which I have become addicted. The bondage in any false self is the bondage of having to keep up the illusion. I am not simply an overachieving good boy. I am not my accomplishments. The things I can do or have done do not make me special. In fact, the attempt to define myself by my accomplishments is as boringly common as it gets!

My compulsive pursuit of accomplishments and the respect of people who are important to me suffocates the life of my true self. It binds and inhibits my growth and restricts my freedom. It is important for me to remember that I am a human being, not a human doing. My worth lies in who I am, not what I can do or how I am seen by others. This is the truth of my existence.

## A DIVINE BATTLE WITH THE FALSE SELF

If Jesus was—as Christians believe—both fully man and fully God, he too had to battle with the false self. He too must have been tempted by false ways of being and excessive attachments to his personal style. In his humanity, his identity in the love of the Father could not have been obvious from the first moments of consciousness as an infant. He had to find himself and in so doing must have been tempted by many false ways of living his life.

We know this to be true because we have a record of some of those temptations. Pennington suggests that the well-known account of the temptation of Jesus in the wilderness (Matthew 4:1-11) is best understood as his struggles with three major potential false selves.[7]

After forty days of fasting, Jesus would have been ravenous. The first attempted seduction of the tempter was to turn stones into bread—a temptation to power. But Jesus said no to the invitation to establish his identity on the basis of his doing, particularly doing something that was independent of submission to the authority of God. Jesus had, Pennington notes, "a better food"—the Word of God (Matthew 4:4).

Then the tempter invited him to throw himself from the top of the temple into the crowds below, so they would immediately recognize him as the Messiah. Again Jesus rejected the temptation. He chose not to base his identity on prestige. And in so doing he took a further step to anchor his identity in the Father, not in what people thought of him.

Finally the tempter offered him all the kingdoms of the world. But once again Jesus rejected the offer, refusing to find his identity in possessions. He knew himself in terms of poverty of spirit and the loving will of the Father. He knew, therefore, that power was a poor substitute for this.

Jesus knew who he was in God. He could therefore resist temptations to live out of a false center based on power, prestige or possessions. By resisting these false ways of being, Jesus was moving toward an identity grounded in his relationship to the Father—an identity in which his calling became obvious as he came to understand who he really was.

## Coming out of Hiding

Every moment of every day of our life God wanders in our inner garden, seeking our companionship. The reason God can't find us is that we are hiding in the bushes of our false self. God's call to us is gentle and persistent: "Where are you? Why are you hiding?"

The more we identify with our psychologically and socially constructed self, the more deeply we hide from God, ourselves and others. But because of the illusory nature of the false self, most of the time we are not aware that we are hiding. Coming out of hiding requires that we embrace the vulnerabilities that first sent us scurrying for cover. As long as we try to pretend that things are not as they are, we choose falsity. The first step out of the bushes is always, then, a step toward honesty with our self.

We all tend to fashion a god who fits our falsity. If my false self is built on an image of moral rectitude, I will tend to bolster this by casting God in the same light. Or if my investment is in an image of self as whimsical, spontaneous and playful, it is almost inevitable that I develop a picture of God painted with these same colors. Having first created a self in the image of our own making, we then set out to create the sort of a god who might in fact create us. Such is the perversity of the false self.

Coming out of hiding is accepting God on God's own terms. Doing so is the only route to truly being our unique self-in-Christ.

If this is your desire, take a few moments to do two things.

First, ask God to help you see what makes you feel most vulnerable and most like running for cover. It may be conflict. Or perhaps it is failure, pain, emotional upset or loss of face. Allow yourself to feel the distress that would be present if you did not avoid these things. Then, listening to God's invitation to come out of the bushes in which you are hiding, step out and allow God to embrace you just as you are.

Second, prayerfully reflect on the image of your self to which you are most attached. Consider how you like to think about yourself, what you are most proud of about yourself. Ask God to help you see the ways you use these things to defend against feelings of vulnerability. And then ask God to prepare you to trust enough to let go of these fig leaves of your personal style.

There is an alternative to the false self. And it takes less energy and work. The way of being that is based on our life in Christ is a way of truth that leads to our vocation and to our deepest possible fulfillment.

# six

# Becoming Your True Self

*T*he true self is the exact opposite of all that I have described as the false self. The true self is who, in reality, you are and who you are becoming. It is not something you need to construct through a process of self-improvement or deconstruct by means of psychological analysis. It is not an object to be grasped. Nor is it an archetype to be actualized. It is not even some inner, hidden part of you. Rather, it is your total self as you were created by God and as you are being redeemed in Christ. It is the image of God that you are—the unique face of God that has been set aside from eternity for you.

We do not find our true self by seeking it. Rather, we find it by seeking God. For as I have said, in finding God we find our truest and deepest self. The anthropological question (Who am I?) and the theological question (Who is God?) are fundamentally inseparable.[1] It is by losing our self in God that we discover our true identity.

There is no true life apart from relationship to God. Therefore there can be no true self apart from this relationship. The foundation of our identity resides in our life-giving relationship with the Source of life. Any identity that exists apart from this relationship is an illusion.

| The False Self | The True Self |
|---|---|
| Security and significance achieved by what we have, what we can do and what others think of us | Security and significance achieved by being deeply loved by God |
| Happiness sought in autonomy from God and in attachments | Fulfillment found in surrender to God and living our vocation |
| Identity is our idealized self (who we want others to think we are) | Identity is who we are—and are becoming—in Christ |
| Achieved by means of pretense and practice | Received as a gift with gratitude and surrender |
| Maintained by effort and control | Maintained by grace |
| Embraces illusion as a means of attempting to become a god | Embraces reality as the place of meeting and being transformed by God |

## AN IDENTITY GROUNDED IN GOD

Because the true self can exist only in relation to God, we see its clearest expression in the one person who lived his whole life closely and consistently in relation to God—Jesus. Jesus is the True Self who shows us by his life how to find our self in relation to God. The self we find hidden in Christ is our true self, because Christ is the source of our being and ground of our true identity (1 Corinthians 15:22).

No one is born with an identity, and Jesus was no exception. Some people worry that an exploration of the humanity of Jesus compromises his divinity. But being fully man and fully God means that he was nothing less than fully human.[2] And being fully human meant that he, like all humans, had to discover who he was.

Even Jesus had to find his way, his self. What do we know about how he did so?

The Gospels tell us remarkably little about his childhood. Apart from a few stories of visitors during infancy and the family's movements to and from Egypt, they present only one event in the approximately thirty years between his birth and baptism in which his actions are described—his visit to the temple at age twelve. But before we consider this event, let us speculate about what it must have been like to be Jesus in the years before that public incident.

All children first find themselves in relation to their parents. Jesus would have been no different. Mary was, of course, a woman apart from all others—"highly favored" by God and "of all women . . . the most blessed" (Luke 1:29, 42). Her humble surrender to the will of God—"let what you have said be done to me" (Luke 1:38)—set the stage for Jesus' own learning of life lived in relation to God. And over time, Jesus undoubtedly began to internalize Mary's steadfast confidence in the trustworthiness of God's love. Over time Jesus would have also absorbed Mary's deep conviction that he was the "Son of the Most High" (Luke 1:32). He would have grown up hearing the stories of the remarkable events of his birth and early years. He would have heard of the visits of the shepherds and wise men, and of the prophecies of Simeon and Anna on the day he was circumcised. He would know that his family viewed him as the promised and long-awaited savior, the Christ who would bring salvation to Israel and light to the pagans (Luke 2:32).

Jesus could have responded to these expectations by developing a smug sense of entitlement that would lead him to lord it over his relatives, friends and even parents. Being the Son of God could have been a power trip of disastrous proportions. But we don't see this. Instead his emerging sense of fundamental relatedness to God led him to a loving dependence on and surrender to God. The event at age twelve gives us a glimpse at the self that was developing at this point.

As recorded in Luke 2:41-50, this incident revolved around the annual trip made by Jesus and his family to the temple for the feast of the Passover. At the conclusion of the feast, Mary and Joseph left with the family caravan, thinking that Jesus was with his cousins. A day later, discovering that he was not in the group, they returned to Jerusalem to try and find him. After three panicky days of looking they finally found him at the temple, "sitting among the doctors, listening to them, and asking them questions" (v. 46).

Seemingly surprised by his parents' concern, Jesus responded in a way that said a great deal about his understanding of who he was: "Why were you looking for me? . . . Did you not know that I must be busy with my Father's affairs?" (v. 49).

Jesus had come to think about himself in relation not simply to earthly parents but to his heavenly Parent. And he was beginning to understand that this latter, most fundamental aspect of his identity was the soil out of which his calling was to emerge. He was beginning to understand that his Father's affairs were his affairs, his Father's priorities his priorities.

Jesus would later ask his disciples who people thought he was and who they thought he was (Matthew 16:13-20). This would have been a dangerous question if he had not already been clear on the answer. Jesus did not merely accept the identity that others offered him. Had he done so he would have, like us, been pulled in many different directions.

Judas, among others, hoped he would be a political savior from the oppression of the Romans. Others saw him as a prophet. These and numerous other potential identities were all available as distractions from Jesus' true self. But he did not look to the expectations of others to understand who he was. Instead he looked to his relationship with God.

The clarity of thought and action that would later characterize Jesus' public ministry came from his years of preparation in solitude and anonymity. The core of that preparation was meeting God in the secret place of his inner self. It was through meeting God in places of solitude that Jesus discovered his identity and grew in intimacy with God.

Jesus gave glory to God by being himself—deeply, truly, consistently. Thomas Merton says that "to be a saint means to be myself."[3] Sanctity is finding our hidden and true self in Christ and living out the life that flows from this self in surrender to the loving will and presence of our heavenly Father. In this, Christ leads many sons and daughters to the Father and to the freedom of being our true self.

## VOCATION

But identity is not static. It always gives direction to how we live our life. The discovery of our true self does not simply produce freedom. It also generates vocation.

*Vocation* is the older, more theologically rooted word for what we sometimes today refer to as "calling." Both point us in the same direction—toward a purpose of being that is grounded in God rather than in our self. Our vocation, like our self, can be understood only in relation to the One Who Calls.

We can understand God's call to us at a number of levels. First, we are called to be human beings. In *Becoming Human*, Jean Vanier reminds us of the fundamental importance of this call to discover and live out our shared humanity. He describes it is "a journey from loneliness to a love that grows in and through belonging," a love that "liberates us from self-centred compulsions and inner hurts . . . that finds its fulfillment in forgiveness and in loving those who are our enemies."[4] This, and nothing less, is what is involved in the call to become fully human.

A second level of calling is to be Christians. This builds on the first by showing us the route to the fulfillment of our humanity. Genuine Christ-following will always make us more, not less, human. We know something is seriously wrong if it does not. Jesus Christ, the perfect God-Man, bridges the chasm between God and humanity. By becoming fully human, Jesus leads us to the fulfillment of our humanity. By being fully God, he leads us to God.

But we can also think of our calling in terms of our mission in the world, the way of living out our uniqueness within the more general call to become fully human as we follow Jesus toward union with God. Gordon Smith notes that—much bigger than a career, job or occupation—our unique calling will be based on our gifts and abilities, will grow out of our deepest desires, and will always involve some response to the needs of the world.[5]

The Christian concept of vocation derives its meaning from the belief in "a creator God who molds humanity and all nature with loving intent, seeking the flourishing and fulfillment of all created things."[6] Our calling is therefore the way of being that is both best for us and best for the world. This is what Frederick Buechner means when he states that "the place God calls you to is the place where your deep gladness and the world's deep hunger meet."[7]

Our vocation is always a response to a Divine call to take our place in the kingdom of God. Our vocation is a call to serve God and our fellow humans in the distinctive way that fits the shape of our being. In one way or another, Christian calling will always involve the care of God's creation and people. This realigns us to the created world and to our neighbor, moving us from self-centered exploitation to self-sacrificing service and stewardship.

The communal nature of the kingdom of God also draws our attention to the fact that we discover our calling—and, as previously noted, our true self—in community. Here, through the help of others who know us well, we learn to discern our gifts and find our authentic voice and vocation. We are all called to Christ-following and loving service of God and neighbor. But the specific call that is rooted in your unique identity, gifts and personality will be found as you come to know both God and self in Christian community.

To live apart from a sense of calling by God is to live a life oriented simply to our own choices about who we want to be and what we want to do. Calling brings freedom and fulfillment because it orients us toward something bigger than self.

## A Vocation Grounded in Identity

Just as Jesus had to work out his identity, so too he had to discern his calling. Like us, he faced the demand to work out with God the truth of his being. We have seen how this was developing at age twelve. The next glimpse the Gospels provide of him was approximately eighteen years later, when he presented himself to his cousin John for baptism. Here we begin to see the unfolding of his vocation.

John was not happy about the idea of baptizing his cousin Jesus. He had long viewed Jesus as the Messiah and had found his own calling as the one who prepared the way for Jesus. He argued that Jesus should baptize him, not the other way around. But Jesus was insistent. "Leave it like this for the time being," he said. "It is fitting that we should, in this way, do all that righteousness demands" (Matthew 3:15). John gave in and baptized Jesus.

The feature of this account that I find most striking is Jesus' humility. He knew that he was without sin and did not need the baptism of repentance. But involvement in his Father's affairs included meeting the demands of righteousness. Here was no megalomaniac who was unable to stoop to submit to his humble and rather eccentric cousin. He was able to submit to his cousin, however, because he was first prepared to submit to the will of God. Nothing mattered more than that.

The way of the true self is always the way of humility. Pride and arrogance move us toward our false self, but humility and love allow us to live the truth of our being. Jesus was on his way to knowing his calling because he was perfectly and completely the True Self.

Perhaps the most revealing of the Gospel accounts about Jesus' understanding of his vocation is that presented in Luke 4. Arriving in Nazareth one sabbath in the first days of his public ministry, Jesus did as was his custom and went to the synagogue. Standing up to read, he was handed the scroll of the prophet Isaiah. Unrolling the scroll, he selected and read the following words:

> The spirit of the Lord has been given to me,
> for he has anointed me.
> He has sent me to bring the good news to the poor,
> to proclaim liberty to captives
> and to the blind new sight,
> to set the downtrodden free,
> to proclaim the Lord's year of favor. (Luke 4:18-19)

As he finished, every eye in the synagogue was on Jesus. The unspoken question in everyone's mind was *Who is this man who dares to take upon himself the mantle of the Messiah?*

Jesus heard the unspoken question and answered it with shocking directness: "This text is being fulfilled today even as you listen" (Luke 4:22).

How had Jesus come to discover that he was to be the fulfillment of the promises of the Old Testament? What could have ever produced such astounding confidence to lead him to assert that the text that had been read so often in synagogues throughout Israel referred to him? The answer lies in part in what he had been doing in the days preceding this remarkable incident.

This bold assertion of vocation came immediately on the heels of Jesus' forty days of temptation in the wilderness (Luke 4:1-13). Jesus' understanding of his vocation came out of wrestling with God, himself and the devil in the solitude of the wilderness.[8] Resisting the temptations to a false self based on power, prestige or possessions, Jesus chose his true identity as the deeply loved Son of God. His identity was not an issue. This is why he was also not distracted by the critics who tried to dismiss him as being merely Joseph's son (Luke 4:23). Jesus knew who his Father was, and as a consequence he knew what his calling was—to do the will of the Father.

Nothing was more central to Jesus' understanding of his calling than to do God's will. Describing a dependence on God that could appear to be unhealthily infantile, Jesus said that he could do nothing whatsoever by himself because his aim was not to do his own will but the will of God (John 5:30). Doing God's will was so central to who he was that on another occasion he described his kin as those who, like him, obeyed the will of the Father. This kinship-of-calling was sufficiently strong that—as in the incident at the temple at age twelve—Jesus risked giving offense to his natural family by affirming the priority of his heavenly family. Nothing took primacy for Jesus over surrender to the loving will of the Father, even the subservient obligation of love of family and neighbor.

Our call, like Jesus' call, is to live out our life in truth and in dependence on the loving will of the Father. As was the case for Jesus, the discernment of this call must always involve wrestling with God, our self and the devil in the solitude of our private wilderness. And as for Jesus, this discernment must always occur in the light of our present life circumstances. This means that attentiveness to God's call is a lifelong matter.

Jesus' understanding of his calling continued to develop right to the point of his death. He had been predicting his death since early in his ministry (Mark 8:31). So in one sense it was not a surprise to him as he saw it approaching. However, as things began to close in around him in the Garden of Gethsemane, he may have found himself doubting that he had read God's will correctly. Perhaps he wondered: *Surely this couldn't be God's plan! Surely a premature death just after starting my public ministry could not be the eternal intention of my existence!* But never faltering, Jesus' words were the same: "Let it be as you, not I, would have it" (Matthew 26:39). His unshakable trust was in God. Nothing, he knew, could be more important than doing God's will. This was the reason he was on earth.

Too often we think of God's call (or our vocation) solely in terms of what we do. People speak of being called to the ministry or feeling called to work in healthcare or teaching. However, while doing will always be involved, vocation is much more than our occupation. It is the face of Christ we are called from eternity to show to the world. It is who we are called to be.

## LIVING THE TRUTH OF OUR UNIQUENESS

As an adolescent, I had a lurking fear that God was going to call me to be a missionary, like the uncle I was named after and the heroes of my family and our church who received much visible admiration. God's will was presented more in terms of what I did than of who I was. And the place where I was pointed to find this will was external. It was the Bible.

Without deemphasizing the value of the Bible in knowing my calling, I have come to understand an even more basic place in which God's will for me has been communicated. That is in the givens of my being. My temperament, my personality, my abilities, and my interests and passions all say something about who I was called to be, not simply who I am. If I really believe that I was created by God and invited to find my place in his kingdom, I have to take seriously what God had already revealed about who I am.

I cannot, for example, imagine God giving me my interest in ideas and not making this an important part of the place I am called to fill in the kingdom. Thoughts have always been my inner companions. I seek dialogue as a way to explore and organize these imperfectly formed parts of my inner architecture. And I gravitate toward writing as an extension of this. Similarly, my interest in people—particularly in meeting and understanding them in their depths—was part of my attraction to psychology and subsequent interest in spiritual direction. And my longstanding interest in the dynamics of the soul has been a central part of finding my way toward a calling in soul care.

My calling is not simply to be a lecturer, writer or psychologist. It is to be a kingdom servant of Yahweh. But the way I am to do that is grounded in the self that God created. And that self has directed me toward the understanding and promotion of the well-being of the inner life of persons. That is why David Benner was created, and that is the context within which I am called to live out the truth of my existence in dependence on God.

While the first revelation of our calling is in the givens of our being, it is important to note that God's will for us does not always grow naturally out of our wishes. Jonah is a good example of someone whose calling was diametrically opposite to his superficial desires. Moses didn't like public speaking, and Gideon didn't feel courageous. Even Jesus didn't look forward to being crucified! This is the discipline of doing what we don't want to do but know we should. Doing so can also be transforming.

God sometimes calls people to a cause not born of their own abilities or most superficial desires. But his call is always absolutely congruent with our destiny, our truest self, our identity and the shape of our being.

We are all called to live the truth of our uniqueness. Divine creativity has never involved a production assembly line. The results of God's creative acts are never less than original and truly unique works of art. You and I are no exception.

But God does not only create us in uniqueness. God meets us in our uniqueness. Think, for example, of the quite different ways Jesus encounters people in the Gospels. Some are simply invited to follow him, some are engaged in Socratic dialogue, some are given provocative parables as answers to questions, some are healed, some are told their sins are forgiven. There has never been one standard way to meet God.

God meets us in our individuality because God wants to fulfill that individuality. God wants us to follow and serve in and through that individuality. God doesn't seek to annihilate our uniqueness as we follow Christ. Rather, Christ-following leads us to our truest self.

The spiritual life of one person should never be a carbon copy of that of another. Peter and John had quite different personalities and quite different transformational journeys as they followed Jesus. Mary and Martha, two sisters whom Jesus loved deeply, each expressed their love for him uniquely. And he received both, not discouraging Martha from busying herself in service, simply encouraging her to not fret in doing so (Luke 10:38-42).

God's will for us is that we live out the harmonious expression of our gifts, temperament, passions and vocation in truthful dependence on God. Nothing less than this is worthy of being called our true self. Nothing less than this will lead to our deepest fulfillment. And nothing less than this will allow us to show the face of Christ to the world that we have been called from eternity to show.

## OUR CALLING, OUR FULFILLMENT

Christ's way to self-fulfillment is not like any way we could ever have imagined. His way involves losing our life so that we might find it, dying so that we might live. His way is always the way of the cross. Death always precedes new life.

Our happiness is important to God. But what he desires for us is infinitely more than the superficial feelings that come from pursuing happiness directly. What he wants to give us is the deep joy that comes from finding our self in Christ—that is, being poor in spirit, mournful, meek, hungry for righteousness, merciful, pure in heart, a peacemaker, persecuted for the sake of the kingdom (Matthew 5:1-10).

Our fulfillment is also important to God. But the self he wants to fulfill is not the self of our autonomous existence. Nor is it any of the false selves of our own creation. It is our truest and deepest self.

Happiness and fulfillment are blessings that come from surrender to the loving will of God. Both are idolatrous if pursued directly. Both are also easily a distraction from our true destiny, our calling in Christ. This is the only self within which we will ever be able to find absolute authenticity.

It is like putting on a perfectly custom-tailored dress or suit after wearing clothes made for other people. Our self-in-Christ is a self that fits perfectly because it is completely us. It is a self that allows us to be free of all anxiety regarding how we should be and who we are. And it allows us to be absolutely our self—unique not by virtue of our strivings for individuality but profoundly original simply because that is who and what we are.

God's call to our fulfillment is therefore a call to take our place in his grand restoration agenda of making all things new in Christ. Our vocation is grounded in the self that from eternity God has willed that we be. Our calling is to become that self and then to serve God and our fellow human beings in the particular ways that will represent the fulfillment of that self. Our identity is not simply a possession. It is a calling.

Paradoxically, our fulfillment lies in the death of our own agendas of fulfillment. It also lies in the crucifixion of all our ego-centered ways of living apart from complete surrender to God. It does not lie, then, in any of the places we would expect to find it. Christ's way always turns our ways upside down. But it is only in the upside-down world of Christ's kingdom that we will ever find the self we were called from eternity to be and the God we were created to serve. In God alone is the truth of our being.

## THE NEXT STEP

The ideas and ideals of this chapter are big. Postmodern cynics smirk at the notion that there is a way of being for each of us that is truth. But if our identity is grounded in Truth, the self we find there will be, for each of us, the unique truth that is our vocation.

It remains to make these big ideals practical. I assume that having read thus far, you have already done some of the preliminary work of knowing yourself and God and of meeting God in your depths. None of us ever finishes with this work, so don't fail to read on simply because you know there is more work to be done in this area. Nor do we ever wait until this work is completed to figure out our vocation. The discernment of our vocation is an ongoing, lifelong process. It is learning to live the truth of our being, not simply fill certain roles or accomplish certain expectations.

You may feel that your calling has been clear for many years. You may have already answered God's call to some form of ministry. Or you may feel you have already found your calling in your work. But at some point in the near future, take some time to review this call with God—not to determine whether you should change what you are doing but to help you live the truth of your life with even more focus and passion. Periodic times of prayerful review of calling can be a great aid in keeping our Christ-following personalized, up to date and in focus.

On the other hand, you may still be struggling with what your calling in life is. You may feel that rather than a review, what you need is for God to finally and clearly reveal your vocation. If so, approach the suggestions that follow with patience. Remember to not confuse your vocation and your job or career. And don't assume that you have not already been living out that vocation. Often looking back at who we have been helps us discern who we are called to be.

Regardless of your confidence about your calling or your sense of progress in the development of your true self, let me suggest two things for prayerful review.

1. Set aside some time to meditate on the Gospel account of Jesus' trip to the temple at age twelve (Luke 2:41-50). Conduct an imaginary conversation with Jesus, asking him where he found his clear sense of his identity. Listen to him speak and watch him act. See what you can learn from his knowing of himself in relationship to God. Then pick up this conversation with Jesus as you meditate on his public declaration of his calling in the synagogue as recorded in Luke 4:16-22.

2. Prayerfully write out a mission statement for your life. Think back over your life to this point, reviewing the givens of your being and seeking to discern calling within them. Add to this any direct leadings of God that you believe yourself to have received. Begin your written statement with the words "Called to . . ." and allow it to reflect what you feel to be the reason you were created and the unique face of Christ you have been called to be. Discuss this with someone who knows you well and whom you trust, seeking their perspective but not adopting it as your own unless it is confirmed by prayer and careful reflection.

# Identity and
# the Spiritual Journey

*C*hristian spirituality is a transformational journey. It is taking on the mind and heart of Christ as we recognize Christ as the deepest truth of our being. It is not just becoming like Christ but actualizing the Christ who is in us. It is a journey toward union with God. And if these things don't challenge and ultimately transform the very foundations of our identity, we have not yet gone very far on this journey.

## IDENTIFYING YOUR IDENTITY

Our identity is something we take for granted. We may have some memory of how much we struggled to find a way of being in the world as adolescents and assume that once we settled into early adulthood, the issue of our identity was behind us. But this confuses our persona and our identity. Our persona is how we want others to see us. Our identity is how we see and understand our self. This continues to develop through life. If it didn't retain some fluidity, transformation of our self would not be possible. However, because human transformation at its core is the transformation of identity, all other changes that are part of the transformational journey flow from this.

But what is our identity at any point in time? Although it could sound like a tautology, our identity is based on the things with which we most identify. For example, if we identify with power, our identity will be based on our sense of our power. Or if we identify with success, our identity will be based on our sense of our success.

To get a sense of your identity, notice how you introduce yourself to others. Perhaps you describe yourself in terms of your work, your accomplishments, your family or your beliefs. Each in turn gives us a snapshot of your identity. Each also, of course, reflects something of your persona (how you want others to see you), but more importantly each provides a good window in on how you see yourself.

Once you get your identity in focus and begin to look more carefully at it, you will also notice how it reflects what psychologists call dis-identifications—that is, people you definitely do not want to be like. Often these start with one or both of your parents, but they need not be limited to one's family or childhood. When noticing a dis-identification you will often be struck by the amount of energy and strength of emotions that are associated with this. This sort of investment of emotional energy always betrays a strong attachment—whether this is an attachment of identification or dis-identification. Both powerfully shape our sense of self.

Observing and reflecting even more deeply on your identity you will often notice that it rests on an even deeper foundation. At its core the default identity for most people in the West is that of a separate self. There are, of course, an infinite number of places where we can draw the line between self and non-self. Extreme separation of self involves a profound existential sense of alienation and aloneness. But this is softened as the boundary is re-drawn to define self in terms that take account of family or those who share my gender, sexual orientation, ethnicity, politics, religion, theology or something else.

But the transformation of identity that I am describing when I talk about realizing that my deepest self is Christ-in-me is more than an enlargement of these boundaries. It involves something much more profound. It challenges the distinction between self and non-self that we all tend to live with. And it profoundly challenges the sense of separateness that typically forms the foundation of our identity.[1]

## THE TRANSFORMATION OF IDENTITY

The journey into God that is at the core of Christ-following leads to the discovery that the foundation of our very being is our being-in-God. Increasingly we come to recognize the inextricable interconnection of our self-in-God and God's self-in-us. This doesn't involve either a loss of our self or becoming God. It involves becoming more and more fully the truth of our being in God. While our self is not God, it is the place where we meet God. There can therefore be no genuine spiritual transformation if we seek some external meeting place. God's intended home is our heart, and it is meeting God in the depths of our soul that transforms us from the inside out. This is why the self is so important in the Christian transformational journey. It must be encountered, not bypassed. It must be embraced and deeply known if it is to be transformed.

Some approach Christian spirituality as a quest to know God. But this is only part of the story. The whole story demands that our focus be as much about knowing the truth of our self as it is about knowing the truth of God, and the knowing of the self that is involved in Christian spirituality is the knowing of self in relation to God. And the knowing of God's self that is at the transformational core of Christian spirituality is a knowing of God in relation to my self.

The mystery of the Christian gospel is that our deepest, truest self is not what we think of as our own separate self but the self that is one with Christ. This is the reason that the self that embarks on the journey of Christ-following is not the self that arrives. The self that begins the spiritual journey is the self of our own creation, the self we thought ourselves to be. This is the self that dies on the journey. The self that arrives is the self that was loved into existence by Divine Love. This is the person we were destined from eternity to become—the I that is hidden in the "I AM."

## CONTINUING THE JOURNEY

As you look back, I hope that you can see how the self that began your own spiritual journey is not the self that now continues it. I also hope that you have come to better know both the "I AM" and your own "I that is hidden in Christ." And because you are reading this book, I trust that you continue to be open to participating as fully as you possibly can in this transformational journey.

Let me therefore offer some concluding words of advice to help you do so.

1. Take some time to reflect on what you have learned of yourself and God through the process of this book. Many people tell me that they give it a second much slower reading, and often a third or fourth. Make these subsequent readings (even if they are just a review of your highlights or margin comments) more contemplative and less about acquisition of knowledge. Allow the Spirit to guide you to what should get you rather than you get it. Make space to reflect on what gets you and prayerfully ponder your response.

2. Watch for opportunities to talk with someone you trust about your discoveries. If you are not reading the book to prepare for a pre-established discussion group, see if you might be able to find a few others to join you in such a discussion. Give them time for

a first reading while you review it and the reflection questions in the Appendix, and then meet as a group to help each of you process the book and more importantly support each other in responding to the invitations that the Spirit is presenting to you.

3. Make your prayer the prayer of St. Augustine: *"Novem te, novem me"* (May I know you, may I know myself).[2] This is a profoundly Christian prayer, because it takes us to the heart of the Christian transformational journey. Watch for opportunities to advance both knowings each and every day. Take time at the end of each day to reflect on the day and then notice your reactions to the experiences of the day. Notice also the movements in your spirit across the day, and the moods and other subtle changes in your inner experience. Give them prayerful reflection, asking for the Spirit of God to help you see where God was in these moments and experiences. Ask also for the help of the Spirit in understanding the invitations that God was offering you for deeper knowing of your self and God's self through each. And then end each time of brief prayerful pondering with thanks to God for this day's gifts of presence.

4. The cultivation of your own presence is another powerful way in which you can come to better know yourself and God. Don't think of presence as a time to think about your day or analyze your self, but rather as a time to step aside from thinking and simply be present. Presence to anything or anyone starts with presence to your self. But the presence you experience will always involve a participation in the Presence that is the ground in which you exist and which makes any small gift of presence that you receive possible. God is always present and your presence—even when you are not thinking of anything, including God—is presence to Divine Presence. But because times of intentional presence involve the quieting of the mind

(particularly your thoughts), it involves a higher degree of openness to contemplative knowing. Presence is the place where we experience this deeper knowing. It is therefore the place in which we encounter both self and God in ways that are less cluttered by preconceptions and judgments. It is a place where we encounter our being and the Ground of All Being.

5. Meditation or contemplation is the practice of presence.[3] So if you are already practicing contemplative prayer or other contemplative or meditative practices, you are already practicing presence. All take you to the deeper places within your self where you can know self and God, not simply know about them. Make space for this contemplative knowing that accompanies presence. Without it, your knowing of the things we have discussed in this book will always be shallow and limited. With it, you offer consent to the deeper levels of transformation that we have been discussing in these first two books in the trilogy and which will be our focus in the third book, *Desiring God's Will*, where we will examine the transformation of will and desire.

6. Most importantly, don't slip into thinking of these things I am encouraging you to do as ways of generating knowing of your self or God. This would be a return to the spirituality of self-improvement. What you are inviting by following these suggestions is the grace of knowing. This is always a gift of God. But you have to turn up to receive and open this gift. My suggestions are therefore simply ways in which you turn up with openness to Grace. They are ways in which you offer your consent to the inflow of Grace that you seek. They are things Christians have done across the whole rich history of our tradition as they have sought to open themselves to God in order to know both themselves and God. They are therefore spiritual practices that can be trusted.

*Appendix*

# For Reflection and Discussion

*N*o one gets very far on the path of Christian spirituality without two things—space for contemplative reflection and engagement with others who share the journey. I have already invited some of the former by offering suggestions for reflection at the end of each chapter. This was a way of encouraging you to take the necessary time to ponder what you were reading.

Now that you have finished the book let me invite you to once again take time to reflect on what you have read as I offer questions and suggestions suitable for both individuals and groups. I have organized these around two types of groups. The first is a group that meets for six sessions of forty-five minutes, each session discussing one or more chapters. This is followed by a suggested framework for a group that meets only once for seventy-five to ninety minutes for a discussion of the book as a whole. If you are using this Appendix for your own reflection and do not anticipate being part of a group discussion, you can draw from either of these sets of questions.

# A Six-Session Discussion Guide
## to *The Gift of Being Yourself*

*~ Session One ~*

### Preface: Identity and Authenticity *AND* Chapter 1: Transformational Knowing of Self and God

1. In preparation for this first session let me suggest that you go back through the preface and chapter 1 and make a note of your favorite quotes. Perhaps you have already done this by marking your book, but if so I would still encourage you to mark the two to three selections that most affected you. As you introduce yourself to the others at the start of this first session, share the one quote that most deeply affected you and tell the group how you responded to it.

2. Let me take you back to the epigraph at the beginning of this book. It is a quote from Thomas Merton: "There is only one problem on which all my existence, my peace, and my happiness depend: to discover myself in discovering God. If I find Him I will find myself and if I find my true self I will find Him." What would you say is the one thing on which your existence, peace and happiness depend? What makes it hard for you to believe what Merton says in this quote? What difference would it make to your life if what he says were true?

3. Chapter 1 suggests, "Body and soul contain thousands of possibilities out of which you can build many identities. But in only one of these will you find your true self that has been hidden in Christ from all eternity. Only in one will you discover your unique vocation and deepest fulfillment." Do you agree that you have a hidden identity that is not yours to construct but discover, and that this identity is your self-in-God? What are the alternate identities that you have been most invested in? Dag Hammarskjöld argues that you will never find this "until you have excluded all those superficial and fleeting possibilities of being and doing with which you toy out of curiosity or wonder or greed, and which hinder you from casting anchor in the experience of the mystery of life." How does this speak to your search for the truth of your being?

4. Do you agree that the quest for our uniqueness is a sacred quest that has an important place to play in Christian spirituality? Why is this notion a threat to some who seem to assume that as we become more like Christ we become more like each other? How might you attempt to reconcile these two positions?

5. I suggest in chapter 1 that the transformation of the self can only occur when God and self are both deeply known. Make a counter argument based on transformation of the self being possible simply through deep knowing of God. Then identify the consequences of leaving the self out of Christian spirituality. What dangers do you see of focusing on God while failing to know your self?

6. How much of your knowing of God is "knowing about" (objective, impersonal) as opposed to "knowing of" (subjective, personal, relational)? How would you describe the difference between the two? What is the value of "knowing about" and what are its limitations? What is the value of "knowing of" that

grows out of a relationship to the object that is known, and what (if any) limitations might be associated with it?

7. In chapter 1, reread the discussion found in the section "Peter's Transformational Knowledge" about Peter's spiritual journey and the slow process of transformation it involved, and reflect on how it matches or does not match your own journey. What do you learn from it? What does it suggest to you about the interweaving of deepening knowledge of self and God?

8. What are you prepared to name as a personal, direct experience of God? How did it occur and what did it involve? What have you learned about yourself as a result of experienced encounters with God? And what do you know about God as a result of genuine encounter with your self?

*~ Session Two ~*

CHAPTER 2: KNOWING GOD

1. In preparation for this session let me again suggest that you go back through chapter 2 and identify your favorite quotes. To start this second session, share your most important take-away from session 1 and the one quote that most deeply affected you from chapter 2—and how you have responded to it.

2. Reread Vicki's experience and longings as described in the beginning of this chapter. What do you know of her longing? And what do you know of her frustration around the lack of fulfillment of this deep desire? What would you say to her if she was your friend or a participant in your book discussion group?

3. In this chapter, I suggest that, "God has no more stopped being Revelation than God has stopped being Love." Do you agree that God continues to self-reveal? Think about what this means for humans today. What is the relationship between what is revealed of God in the past and what we can know directly and personally of God now? How can we know God, not just know about God? Bring your thoughts and questions about this to the group as you prepare to discuss the implications of following this self-revealing God.

4. How does knowing God differ from knowing humans? In what ways is it similar? What special demands does knowing God make on humans?

5. Those who know the most about direct personal knowing of God (the mystics) tell us that because God is love, God can only be known in and through love. What does it mean to know God by means of the heart (through love), not simply the mind (through thoughts and beliefs)? Which best describes your knowing? What do you know of the limitations of objective knowing of God? How might objective knowing of God support personal experiential knowing?

6. Recall the Thomas Merton quote I share in this chapter: "We must know the truth, we must love the truth we know and we must act according to the measure of our love. Truth is God himself who cannot be known apart from love and cannot be loved apart from surrender to his will." Do you agree? If not, why not? What is the role of surrender and love in knowing God?

7. What was your experience during the Gospel meditation exercise I suggest for Mark 10:17-22? If you haven't done it yet, reread the passage and engage with it as a guided meditation. What value might be in this sort of meditation as a way of engaging with Jesus

and through him, knowing God? What, if anything, makes you uncomfortable about the use of the senses and imagination in this sort of prayerful pondering of a Gospel story?

8. Why is it hard to sense God's presence with you in the midst of the ordinary events of your day? What things help you do so? What have you discovered about God's presence with you even in times of painful, tragic or unwelcome events?

### ~ *Session Three* ~

### CHAPTER 3: FIRST STEPS TOWARD KNOWING YOURSELF

1. In preparation for this session let me again suggest that you go back through chapter 3 and identify your favorite quotes. To start this third session, share your most important take-away from session 2 and the one quote that most deeply affected you from chapter 3—and how you have responded to it.

2. What is your self that is known by God? Do you agree that this is the self that we should be actualizing as we seek to know our truth? How do you get to know this self—not as a theological abstraction to be believed but as the truth of your self to be realized?

3. Do you believe that God loves and knows you with unimaginable depth, persistence and intensity in your personal individuality? If so, looking into God's eyes would involve seeing yourself reflected back—just like an infant gazing up into the loving face of his or her parent. What makes it hard for you to look into God's eyes to see yourself reflected there? What helps make it possible?

4. In this chapter I suggest that an identity grounded in God would mean that when we think of who we are, the first thing that would come to mind is our status as someone who is deeply loved by God. How true is this of you? When you notice what comes to mind when you think of yourself, what do you learn about your identity? What keeps you from knowing your self-in-God?

5. Reread the section "Knowing Yourself as Deeply Loved" where I discuss Jesus' identity. What do you learn about how to ground your sense of self in God from reflecting on how Jesus did this?

6. How could meeting God in the vulnerability of your present realities help you better know the you that God sees when God looks at you? What would help you come to God with more of this vulnerability and more honesty, daring to trust that God is with you in the midst of those present realities you may be trying to escape or minimize?

7. How have you been growing in your acceptance and embracing of the shadow and all the parts of yourself that you have instinctively wanted to ignore? What has helped you welcome these lost parts of self into the family-of-selves that are being woven in you?

8. Do you agree that you cannot know the truth of your self without first accepting the things about yourself that you wish were not true? What dimensions or parts of your self do you have the most trouble acknowledging, naming and embracing? Remember that daring to name them to yourself and others is a first step in your acceptance of them, so dare to take that step. How could the church (or other forms of spiritual community) do a better job of helping us embrace the seemingly unacceptable parts of ourselves?

## ~ *Session Four* ~

### CHAPTER 4: KNOWING YOURSELF AS YOU REALLY ARE

1. In preparation for this session let me again suggest that you go back through chapter 4 and identify your favorite quotes. To start this fourth session, share your most important take-away from session 3 as well as the one quote that most deeply affected you from chapter 4—and how you have responded to it.

2. Reflect on the following quote from Thomas Merton: "There is no greater disaster in the spiritual life than to be immersed in unreality, for life is maintained and nourished in us by our vital relation with reality." How would you rate your own embrace of reality? What keeps you from a total commitment to and acceptance of all of your present life realities? What things help you name and release the illusions that compromise your total commitment to reality?

3. In contrast to my suggestion that our identity should be based on being deeply loved by God, some Christians argue that our identity as Christians must be grounded in the fact that we are sinners. Which end of this polarity best fits with your beliefs? Take some time to discuss these options for identity within the group and consider whether your theology adequately reflects and supports your spirituality.

4. I argue in this chapter that sin is more a matter of ontology (being) than morality (behavior). To be a human is to be a sinner. It is to be broken, damaged goods that carry within our deepest self a fundamental, fatal flaw that masks our original creation goodness. Do you agree? If not, why not? How would you define sin?

5. Reread the discussion of the case of Stuart presented in the section "Getting Behind Sins to Sin." How would you understand his essential problems? How does his story fit with how you define sin? How does it fit with how you approach your spiritual journey?

6. Where do you see yourself in the Enneagram typology based on your reading of what I say in the section "An Ancient Aid to Deep Knowing of Our Sin" or your personal work with it? What, if any, help might (or does) it offer to an understanding and knowing of hidden dimensions of your self that need to be acknowledged before they can be integrated and then transformed? What other tools and processes have you worked with that have helped you know yourself deeply?

7. I end this chapter by suggesting that genuine self-knowledge is available to all who (1) honestly desire it, (2) are willing to prayerfully reflect on their experience and (3) have the courage to meet themselves and God in solitude. Treat each of these requirements as a ten-point scale and rate yourself on this scale for each of the requirements. What does this help you see about where you presently are on your transformational journey?

8. What is the next step that you feel invited to take on your own journey? How do you respond to the invitation to take that step?

### ~ *Session Five* ~

## CHAPTER 5: UNMASKING YOUR FALSE SELF

1. In preparation for this session let me again suggest that you go back through chapter 5 and identify your favorite quotes. To

start this session, share your most important take-away from session 4 and the one quote that most deeply affected you from chapter 5—and how you have responded to it.

2. Do you agree that everything that is false about us arises from our belief that our deepest happiness will come from living life our way, not God's way? If not, what other sources of falsity can you identify? Why do you doubt that God is capable of securing our happiness? In your view, how does that doubt lead to the development and strengthening of a false self?

3. How do you want others to see you? What does this tell you about your assumptions regarding what you think will make you happy and fulfilled? How did this image become more and more the lie you have lived over time? How ready are you to lessen your attachment to it?

4. Basil Pennington suggests that the core of the false self is the belief that my value depends on what I have and what I can do. What additional dimensions of your falsity can you identify after prayerful reflection on your attachment to what you have and what you can do? How would you release that attachment? What do you fear in doing so?

5. Anything that we cling to other than God can represent an inordinate attachment. How do you assess your strongest attachments? Which most likely reflect some degree of an inordinate (or disordered) attachment? What keeps you clinging to them? How do they represent ways of coping with feelings of vulnerability, shame and inadequacy that lie at the core of our false self?

6. Notice your patterns of touchiness and over-reactivity. What help do they offer in better understanding your false ways of being? Now do the same with your compulsions and addic-

tions. Don't be quick to say that you don't have any compulsions or addictions. Remember, addictive dynamics characterize all of us and lie underneath our compulsions.

7. Reread the story of the temptation of Jesus in the wilderness (Matthew 4:1-11) and the discussion of this in the section "A Divine Battle with the False Self." What does prayerful pondering on the way in which Jesus dealt with his temptations to falsity offer you in considering how you might better deal with yours?

8. What invitation do you experience from the Spirit to come out of hiding from God—accepting yourself and God on God's own terms of unconditional love? What are you ready to offer by way of response to this invitation?

### ~ *Session Six* ~

#### CHAPTER 6: BECOMING YOUR TRUE SELF *AND* EPILOGUE: IDENTITY AND THE SPIRITUAL JOURNEY

1. In preparation for this final session let me again suggest that you go back through chapter 6 and the epilogue and identify your favorite quotes. To start this final session, share your most important take-away from session 5 and the one quote that most deeply affected you from chapter 6 and the epilogue—and how you have responded to it.

2. Chapter 6 suggests that ultimately we do not find the truth of our self by analysis and introspection but by losing our self in God. This brings us back to the question of what blocks our surrender to God. Working through the book to this point,

what would you identify as your most important blocks to taking the next step of that surrender? Naming them is a way of embracing your present reality, and this in itself is prayer.

3. In chapter 6, reread the section "An Identity Grounded in God" and reflect on what you can learn about the way Jesus grounded his identity in his relationship to God. Don't be quick to dismiss Jesus as a model for us in this. As the example of what it is to be wholly human, he is the perfect example. What do you learn by reflecting on how he developed and then kept his identity grounded in God?

4. How do you understand your call or vocation? How is this related to being the truth of your self? How might your calling be more integrally related to being and living this truth?

5. In chapter 6, reread the section "A Vocation Grounded in Identity" and reflect on how Jesus connected his vocation and his identity, and consider how his way of living the truth of his uniqueness could be your way.

6. How might both the truth of your identity and your vocation be grounded in your unique set of gifts, temperament, passions, interests, curiosities and deep longings? Reflecting on this is discerning the way in which God's call to you and will for you are already laid down in the uniqueness of your true self.

7. Reflect on the gifts and invitations that you feel have come from the Spirit of God to you through the study and discussion of this book. How will you respond to them? What will be your next step in offering a full-hearted response of "Yes!" to the gift of being yourself?

# A One-Session Discussion Guide to *The Gift of Being Yourself*

1. In preparation for the discussion let me suggest that you go back through the preface and chapter 1 and make a note of your favorite quotes. Perhaps you have already done this by marking your book, but if so I would still encourage you to mark the two to three selections that most affected you. Come prepared to introduce yourself to the others at the start of the meeting by sharing the one quote that most deeply affected you and how you have responded to it.

2. The epigraph at the beginning of this book presents a quote from Thomas Merton: "There is only one problem on which all my existence, my peace, and my happiness depend: to discover myself in discovering God. If I find Him I will find myself and if I find my true self I will find Him." What would you say is the one thing on which your existence, peace and happiness depend? What makes it hard for you to believe what Merton says in this quote? What difference would it make to your life if what he says were true?

3. Do you agree that the quest for our uniqueness is a sacred quest that has an important place to play in Christian spirituality? If you do, why is this notion a threat to some Christians who seem to imply that as we become more like Christ we become more

like each other? How might you attempt to reconcile these two positions?

4. How much of your knowing of God is what I describe in chapter 1 as "knowing about" (objective, impersonal) as opposed to "knowing of" (subjective, personal, relational)? How would you describe the difference between the two? What is the value of "knowing about" and what are its limitations? What is the value of "knowing of" that grows out of a relationship to the object that is known, and what (if any) limitations can you think of associated with it?

5. How does knowing God differ from knowing humans? In what ways is it similar? What special demands does knowing God make on humans?

6. Those who know the most about direct personal knowing of God (the mystics) tell us that because God is love, God can only be known in and through love. What does it mean to know God by means of the heart (through love), not simply the mind (through thoughts and beliefs)? Which best describes your knowing, and why? What do you know of the limitations of objective knowing of God? How might objective knowing of God support personal experiential knowing?

7. What was your experience during the Gospel meditation exercise I suggest for Mark 10:17-22? If you haven't done it yet, reread the passage and engage with it as a guided meditation. What value might be in this sort of meditation as a way of engaging with Jesus and through him, knowing God? What, if anything, makes you uncomfortable about the use of the senses and imagination in this sort of prayerful pondering of a Gospel story?

8. In chapter 3 I suggest that an identity grounded in God would

mean that when we think of who we are, the first thing that would come to mind is our status as someone who is deeply loved by God. How true is this of you? When you notice what comes to mind when you think of yourself, what do you learn about your identity? What keeps you from knowing your self-in-God?

9. How have you been growing in your acceptance and embracing of the shadow and all the parts of yourself that you have instinctively wanted to ignore? What has helped you welcome these lost parts of self into the family-of-selves that are being woven in you?

10. Reflect on the following quote from Thomas Merton: "There is no greater disaster in the spiritual life than to be immersed in unreality, for life is maintained and nourished in us by our vital relation with reality." How would you rate your own embrace of reality? What keeps you from a total commitment to and acceptance of all of your present life realities? What things help you name and release the illusions that compromise your total commitment to reality?

11. In contrast to my suggestion that our identity should be based on being deeply loved by God, some Christians argue that our identity as Christians must be grounded in the fact that we are sinners. Which end of this polarity best fits with your beliefs? Which best fits with your present reality? Take some time to discuss these options for identity within the group and consider whether your theology adequately reflects and supports your spirituality.

12. I suggest in chapter 4 that sin is more a matter of ontology (being) than morality (behavior). To be a human is to be a sinner. It is to be broken, damaged goods that carry within our deepest self a fundamental, fatal flaw that masks our original

creation goodness. Do you agree? If not, why not? How would you define sin?

13. Where do you see yourself in the Enneagram typology based on your reading of what I say in the section "An Ancient Aid to Deep Knowing of Our Sin" or your personal work with it? What, if any, help do you suspect it could offer to an understanding and knowing of hidden dimensions of your self that need to be acknowledged before they can be integrated and then transformed? What other tools and processes have you worked with that have helped you know yourself deeply?

14. Chapter 4 ends with my suggestion that genuine self-knowledge is available to all who (1) honestly desire it, (2) are willing to prayerfully reflect on their experience and (3) have the courage to meet themselves and God in solitude. Treat each of these requirements as a ten-point scale and rate yourself on this scale for each of the requirements. What does this help you see about where you presently are on your transformational journey?

15. Do you agree that everything that is false about us arises from our belief that our deepest happiness will come from living life our way, not God's way? Why do you doubt that God is really capable of securing our happiness? In your view, how does that doubt lead to the development and strengthening of a false self?

16. How do you want others to see you? What does this tell you about your assumptions regarding how you understand what will make you happy and fulfilled? How did this image become more and more the lie you have lived over time? How ready are you to lessen your attachment to it?

17. Basil Pennington suggests that the core of the false self is the belief that my value depends on what I have and what I can do. What additional dimensions of your falsity can you identify

after prayerful reflection on your attachment to what you have and what you can do? How would you release that attachment? What do you fear in doing so?

18. Notice your patterns of touchiness and over-reactivity. What help do they offer in better understanding your false ways of being? Now do the same with your compulsions and addictions. Don't be quick to say that you don't have any compulsions or addictions. Remember, addictive dynamics characterize all of us and lie underneath our compulsions.

19. How do you understand your call or vocation? How is this related to being the truth of your self? How might it be better related to being and living this truth?

20. How might both the truth of your identity and your vocation be grounded in your unique set of gifts, temperament, passions, interests, curiosities and deep longings? Reflecting on this is discerning the way in which God's call to you and will for you are already laid down in the uniqueness of your true self.

21. Reflect on the gifts and invitations that you feel have come from the Spirit of God to you through the study and discussion of this book. How will you respond to them? What is your next step in offering a full-hearted response of "Yes!" to the gift of being yourself?

# Notes

## Preface: Identity and Authenticity

[1]Dag Hammarskjöld, *Markings* (New York: Alfred A. Knopf, 1969), 19.

[2]Thomas Merton, *New Seeds of Contemplation* (New York: New Directions, 1961), 36.

## Chapter 1: Transformational Knowing of Self and God

[1]Thomas à Kempis, *Imitation of Christ*, trans. Clare L. Fitzpatrick (New York: Catholic Book Publishing, 1993), 20.

[2]St. Augustine is quoted in Pierre Pourrat, *Christian Spirituality in the Middle Ages* (London: Burns & Oates, 1924), 291.

[3]John Calvin, *Institutes of the Christian Religion*, 1536 ed., trans. Ford Lewis Battles (Grand Rapids: Eerdmans, 1995), 15.

## Chapter 2: Knowing God

[1]J. I. Packer, *Knowing God*, 20th anniv. ed. (Downers Grove, IL: InterVarsity Press, 1993), 35.

[2]Louis Evely, *That Man Is You* (New York: Paulist, 1964), 15-16.

[3]Packer, *Knowing God*, 27.

[4]Thomas Merton, *The Ascent to Truth* (New York: Harcourt Brace, 1981), 8.

[5]I thank Canon Gray Temple for suggesting this interpretation in his sermon at St. Patrick's Episcopal Church in Atlanta on March 30, 2003.

[6]Carolyn Gratton, *The Art of Spiritual Guidance* (New York: Crossroad, 2000), 40.

[7]R. Paul Stevens, *Down-to-Earth Spirituality: Encountering God in the Ordinary, Boring Stuff of Life* (Downers Grove, IL: InterVarsity Press, 2003), 184.

[8]Ben Johnson describes this as an important dimension of the role of the spiritual director, since we often need the help of another to accomplish this unmasking of the presence of the Divine. I take this thought from his chapter "Spiritual Direction in the Reformed Tradition," in *Spiritual Direction and the Care of Souls*, ed. Gary Moon and David G. Benner (Downers Grove, IL: InterVarsity Press, 2004).

[9]Richard Rohr, *Everything Belongs: The Gift of Contemplative Prayer* (New York: Crossroad, 1999), 28.

[10]David G. Benner, *Sacred Companions: The Gift of Spiritual Friendship and Direction* (Downers Grove, IL: InterVarsity Press, 2002), 113-15.

## CHAPTER 3: FIRST STEPS TOWARD KNOWING YOURSELF

[1]Thomas Merton, *New Seeds of Contemplation* (New York: New Directions, 1961), 34.

[2]J. I. Packer, *Knowing God,* 20th anniv. ed. (Downers Grove, IL: InterVarsity Press, 1993), 41.

[3]Hannah Hurnard, *Kingdom of Love* (Carol Stream, IL: Tyndale House, 1981), 48.

[4]This theme is treated much more extensively in my book *Surrender to Love* (Downers Grove, IL: InterVarsity Press, 2015).

[5]See David G. Benner, *Sacred Companions: The Gift of Spiritual Friendship and Direction* (Downers Grove, IL: InterVarsity Press, 2002), for further discussion of both the importance of spiritual accompaniment and ways of making it happen.

[6]Thomas Merton, *Thoughts in Solitude* (Boston: Shambhala, 1993), 3, 20.

[7]I am thankful to Robert V. Thompson for suggesting the connection between this story and prayer in his sermon "Freedom from the False Self," preached at Lake Street Church of Evanston, IL, February 3, 2002. Although only a small percentage of the Nasrudin folk stories have been translated and written in English, a good introduction to these rather remarkable fables can be found in Idries Shah, *The Pleasantries of the Incredible Mulla Nasrudin* (London: Octagon, 1983).

## CHAPTER 4: KNOWING YOURSELF AS YOU REALLY ARE

[1]Thomas Merton, *Thoughts in Solitude* (Boston: Shambhala, 1993), 3.

[2]James Finley, *Merton's Palace of Nowhere: A Search for God Through Awareness of the True Self* (Notre Dame, IN: Ave Maria, 1978), 27.

[3]Dallas Willard, *The Divine Conspiracy: Rediscovering Our Hidden Life in God* (San Francisco: HarperSanFrancisco, 1998), 35-60.

[4]For a good general introduction to this approach to understanding personality, see Don Richard Riso and Russ Hudson, *The Wisdom of the Enneagram: The Complete Guide to Psychological and Spiritual Growth for the Nine Personality Types* (New York: Bantam Doubleday Dell, 1999). For an explicitly Christian approach to the Enneagram, particularly focusing on its use in understanding one's basic sin, see Richard Rohr, *Enneagram: A Christian Perspective* (New York: Crossroad, 2001), or listen to his discussion of this in *Enneagram: Naming Our Illusions,* a series of six audiotapes produced by Credence Cassettes (Kansas City, MO, 1988).

[5]I am not a fan of systems of personality classification. Often the parts of us that fit within the box are fewer than the parts that do not. And the temptation to relate to others as a "type" is almost irresistible for some people. However, I am a fan of the Enneagram—not as a typology but as a tool to assist in deep knowing of our core sin tendencies. In both my own life and my work with others it has often been extremely helpful.

[6]Although this summary synthesizes the insights of a number of people, it reflects particular indebtedness to the work of Richard Rohr cited in note 4.

[7]Although questionnaires have been developed to help identify types (see Don

Richard Riso and Russ Hudson, *The Riso-Hudson Enneagram Type Indicator* [Stone Ridge, NY: Enneagram Institute, 2000] or www.ennea graminstitute.com/home.asp), the best way to really find yourself within the Enneagram is through prayerful reflection. Because the Enneagram identifies our fundamental illusions, the temptation to flatter ourselves by identifying with statements that fit with how we wish to see ourselves limits the usefulness of questionnaires. Penetrating this defensive web of illusions is a spiritual work that requires time, ruthless honesty and discernment that comes only from attentive openness to the Spirit of God.

### CHAPTER 5: UNMASKING YOUR FALSE SELF

[1]Thomas Keating, *Invitation to Love: The Way of Christian Contemplation* (New York: Continuum, 1998).

[2]Richard Rohr, *Enneagram: Naming Our Illusions,* audiotapes (Kansas City, MO: Credence Cassettes, 1988), tape 1.

[3]James Finley, *Merton's Palace of Nowhere: A Search for God Through Awareness of the True Self* (Notre Dame, IN: Ave Maria, 1978), 31.

[4]M. Basil Pennington, *True Self/False Self* (New York: Crossroad, 2000), 31.

[5]Thomas Merton, *New Seeds of Contemplation* (New York: New Directions, 1961), 35.

[6]Pennington, *True Self/False Self,* 37.

[7]Ibid., 33-34.

### CHAPTER 6: BECOMING YOUR TRUE SELF

[1]Ekman Tam, "Message to the Wounded World: Unmask the True Self—Zen and Merton," *Religious Studies and Theology* 17 (1998): 71-84.

[2]Luke 2:40, 52 affirms the developmental aspects of Jesus' life that assure us that he was in fact human.

[3]Thomas Merton, *New Seeds of Contemplation* (New York: New Directions, 1961), 32.

[4]Jean Vanier, *Becoming Human* (Toronto: Anansi, 1998), 5.

[5]Gordon Smith, *Courage and Calling: Embracing Your God-Given Potential* (Downers Grove, IL: InterVarsity Press, 1999), 33-55.

[6]Alistair Campbell, *Paid to Care* (London: SPCK, 1985), 17.

[7]Frederick Buechner, *Listening to Your Life* (San Francisco: HarperSanFrancisco, 1992), 186.

[8]Juliet Benner, personal communication.

### EPILOGUE: IDENTITY AND THE SPIRITUAL JOURNEY

[1]See David G. Benner, *Spirituality and the Awakening Self* (Grand Rapids: Brazos Press, 2012) for a fuller discussion of the transformation of identity.

[2]St. Augustine, quoted in Pierre Pourrat, *Christian Spirituality in the Middle Ages* (London: Burns & Oates, 1924), 291.

[3]See David G. Benner, *Presence and Encounter* (Grand Rapids: Brazos Press, 2014) for more on the nature of presence and practical guidelines for its cultivation.

# About the Author

*D*r. David G. Benner is an internationally known depth psychologist and transformational coach whose life's work has been directed toward helping people walk the human path in a deeply spiritual way and the spiritual path in a deeply human way. His passion and calling has been the understanding and pursuit of transformation—not merely healing or even growth, but the unfolding of the self associated with a journey of awakening.

David has held faculty appointments at York University, University of Toronto, McMaster University, Redeemer University College, Wheaton College, Psychological Studies Institute at Richmont Graduate University, the Centre for Studies in Religion and Society at University of Victoria and the Living School for Action and Contemplation. He has also served as visiting lecturer at universities in thirty countries and is the author or editor of more than twenty-five books that have been translated into nineteen foreign languages.

Beyond his work in psychology and spirituality David's other principal interests are sailing, cycling, hiking, jazz, good food and soulful conversation. He is married to Juliet Benner, author of *Contemplative Vision: A Guide to Christian Art and Prayer* (InterVarsity Press). They divide their time between Toronto, Canada, and Lima, Peru.

David can be found online at

- www.drdavidgbenner.ca
- www.facebook.com/drdavidgbenner
- Twitter: @drdavidgbenner

# Books by
# David G. Benner

*Presence and Encounter: The Sacramental Possibilities of Everyday Life*
(Brazos Press, 2014)

*Spirituality and the Awakening Self: The Sacred Journey of Transformation*
(Brazos Press, 2012)

*Soulful Spirituality: Becoming Fully Alive and Deeply Human* (Brazos Press,
2011)

*Opening to God: Lectio Divina and Life as Prayer* (InterVarsity Press, 2010)

*Desiring God's Will: Aligning Our Hearts with the Heart of God* (InterVarsity
Press, 2005)

*The Gift of Being Yourself: The Sacred Call to Self-Discovery* (InterVarsity
Press, 2004)

*Spiritual Direction and the Care of Souls: A Guide to Christian Approaches
and Practices,* ed. with Gary Moon (InterVarsity Press, 2004)

*Surrender to Love: Discovering the Heart of Christian Spirituality* (Inter-
Varsity Press, 2003)

*Strategic Pastoral Counseling: A Short-Term Structured Model,* 2nd ed.
(Baker, 2003)

*Sacred Companions: The Gift of Spiritual Friendship and Direction* (Inter-
Varsity Press, 2002)

*Free at Last: Breaking the Bondage of Guilt and Emotional Wounds* (Essence,
1999)

*Care of Souls: Reuniting the Psychological and Spiritual for Christian Nurture
and Counsel* (Baker, 1998)

*Money Madness and Financial Freedom: The Psychology of Money Meanings and Management* (Detselig, 1996)

*Choosing the Gift of Forgiveness*, with Robert Harvey (Baker, 1996)

*Understanding and Facilitating Forgiveness*, with Robert Harvey (Baker, 1996)

*Christian Perspectives on Human Development*, ed. with Leroy Aden and J. Harold Ellens (Baker, 1992)

*Healing Emotional Wounds* (Baker, 1990)

*Counseling and the Human Predicament*, ed. with Leroy Aden (Baker, 1989)

*Psychology and Religion*, ed. (Baker, 1988)

*Psychotherapy and the Spiritual Quest* (Baker, 1988)

*Psychotherapy in Christian Perspective*, ed. (Baker, 1987)

*Christian Counseling and Psychotherapy*, ed. (Baker, 1987)

*Baker Encyclopedia of Psychology*, ed. (Baker, 1985)

## *formatio*
### TRADITION. EXPERIENCE.
### TRANSFORMATION.

Formatio books from InterVarsity Press follow the rich tradition of the church in the journey of spiritual formation. These books are not merely about being informed, but about being transformed by Christ and conformed to his image. Formatio stands in InterVarsity Press's evangelical publishing tradition by integrating God's Word with spiritual practice and by prompting readers to move from inward change to outward witness. InterVarsity Press uses the chambered nautilus for Formatio, a symbol of spiritual formation because of its continual spiral journey outward as it moves from its center. We believe that each of us is made with a deep desire to be in God's presence. Formatio books help us to fulfill our deepest desires and to become our true selves in light of God's grace.